DIAGNOSE SHIFTING FAITH

RETURN TO FAITH IN GOD ALONE AND THRIVE

RAY HAAS

ABSO UNPRO

absolutelyunprofessional.com
Wadsworth, OH

Cover and interior layout and design by Absolutely Unprofessional.

Image credits: Cover photo: Pexels: Artem Yellow Sand Dunes In Desert 15157864; Freepix: Rawpixel.com Medical Stethoscope White Surface 11309538

Print and distribution through ingramspark.com.

First Printing: 2023
979 8-9879116-1-7
Absolutely Unprofessional
Wadsworth, OH 44281
absolutelyunprofessional.com

Contact Ray Haas:
   rayandjenhaas@yahoo.com
plethosglobal.com

TABLE OF CONTENTS

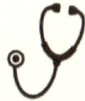

DIAGNOSE

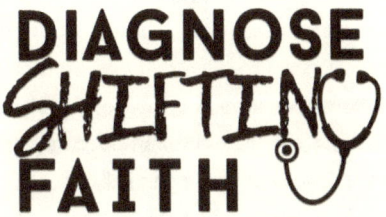

SHIFTING FAITH

Our hearts are so often ensnared by sin that it isn't abnormal for a follower of Jesus—you and me—to either intentionally or unintentionally shift our faith from Christ alone toward another person, group, event, or possession. Yet we don't have to settle for this shift. In fact, in Christ, we're empowered to overcome the sin of shifting faith.

One morning as I met with the Lord in Word and prayer I asked Him why I had become irritated with my wife the night before. He showed me that I had been trusting her for my well-being and not Him alone, that my faith had shifted from Him to my wife. And so when she didn't say or do what pleased me, I grew irritated.

In that highly impactful prayer time it became abundantly clear that had my faith been in God alone I could have graciously asked my wife what she meant by her words and actions instead of walking away irritated. While I couldn't undo my irritable attitude from the evening before, the diagnosis of my shifted faith brought a great deal of peace. Since then, I have viewed irritation as a symptom of my faith having shifted from God to a person, group, event, or possession.

Soon after that morning I began to catalog many symptoms of a shifted faith, some of which we'll touch on in the following chapters (with a more comprehensive list of symptoms in the appendix). I have always known that my faith was to be centered on and sourced in God alone. And I believe most Christians would say the same. However, it wasn't until the Lord brought this spiritual diagnosis to mind that I began looking for symptoms of a shifted faith—before that, even as symptoms escalated, I simply continued trusting people, events, and things not realizing that I was no longer trusting the Lord to meet those particular needs or desires. These days, I'm able to quickly diagnose when my faith has shifted from God and get back to the freedom, peace, and contentment of faith in Him alone.

This book was written so that you might develop a spiritual habit of examining your own life for the symptoms of a shifting faith and then more and more quickly learn to shift your hope and trust back to Jesus, who alone is the source of all our spiritual resources and well-being necessary for a Godly life in Him. The sooner we diagnose the shift, the better it is for us, those around us, and our relationship with God.

As you read, take the time to reflect on the Scripture mentioned and relied upon. These passages help provide the foundation for understanding who God is in relation to our sin and who we are in relation to God's work in overcoming sin in our lives. You'll notice that each chapter ends with a list of passages to reflect on. These passages are mentioned throughout each chapter and then written in full for your benefit. That's right, you're now without excuse for taking the time to dig into the Text more fully. You're welcome!

May the Holy Spirit open your eyes to our greatest danger, sin. And may you run back to Christ, by faith, for Truth and strength time and again as you joyfully fulfill your Christ-centered assignments in this sin-enslaved world.

CHAPTER 1

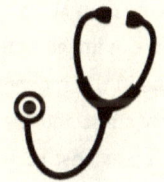

OUR
GREATEST DANGER
IS SIN

Danger Puts Us on High Alert

Three weeks ago I became acutely aware that I was in danger of a major heart attack. Before being alerted to the danger, it was the furthest thing from my mind. You see, I have a good health history, try to eat right, and have exercised diligently since I was 35. At 72, my annual physicals are still good and, to be honest, even improving.

I've often boasted of a low heartbeat which I thought revealed a strong and healthy heart from years of work on an Airdyne stationary bike. I was even doing better on the bike at 72 than at 68. Like I said, I've considered myself to be quite healthy, so you can imagine my surprise when, on January 10, I was awakened at one in the morning with chest and back pain. My t-shirt was soaked on my chest and my head clammy with sweat. I woke my wife and we decided it was best to go to the ER. After a series of blood tests and an ultrasound, I was diagnosed with an incomplete heart attack and advised to stay overnight in the hospital for a minor coronary angiogram procedure. As I closed my eyes in the hospital bed, I had a vision of my arteries being completely cleared. I told the nurse I thought the test the following day would show my arteries all clear.

The angiogram allowed the surgeon to go up an artery in my right arm and see that my heart, valves, and blood vessels all were healthy and clear. Good news.

The next step was to monitor my slow heartbeat for three weeks to determine if this could be the problem. My slow heartbeat became a danger that needed monitoring! Catch that? A sign of being in good physical shape became a danger to avoid—a danger that could take my life. When the three-week monitoring period ended, I was scheduled the next day to go to my post-angiogram, post-monitoring checkup for evaluation and next steps.

The night before my post-checkup, however, I was on high alert once again as I experienced pain in my left arm and shoulder while sitting at my desk in front of my computer. High alert! Immediately I spoke with my wife and showed her the location of all the important papers. I moved my car out of our single-car driveway to allow her to take her vehicle in case of an emergency during the night. I checked the internet for symptoms and then walked around the house, keeping track of the pain.

Next, I had my wife lay hands on me to pray for healing. Soon after, I emailed disciples in Kenya to have them pray for my heart health and a healthy heart rate. As I reached out for prayer, I was reminded by the Lord just how urgent my assignment was.

At the post-checkup I was declared clear of any problems with my heart.

Now, as I sit here, I'm prompted by God to get this most freeing book on diagnosing the symptoms of a shifting faith done. Before my heart set me on high alert, I had told Him I needed urgency, ability, and intimacy (I get lonely doing this work) when He asked me to accept this particular writing assignment.

It seems I now have the urgency, and without a doubt, I know He has the ability (Galatians 2:20; Philippians 4:13).

And on top of that, I have His unwavering intimacy (Matthew 28:20; John 14:21, 23).

The danger of a potential heart attack has grabbed my attention and caused me to get moving on His assignment. The Scriptures assure me of His help as I attempt to do His will and make it clear that He is with me at all times! Did you read the passages I mentioned above? I encourage you to read through each one. In fact, you'll notice I've placed the scriptures in full at the end of this chapter and the chapters following in the order they're referenced. I did that for your convenience and benefit. Be sure to ask the Lord to give you understanding as you take them in.

Connecting the Dots

How does my heart episode address the theme of this chapter—Our Greatest Danger is Sin? We are often unaware of danger until it slaps us in the face, aren't we? I never thought I had a heart problem. Now, I'm on high alert! And just as it was with my heart, there was a time in my life when I didn't think I had a sin problem.

Right out of high school I asked a girl to marry me. I know, I know, that's a pretty big leap for a young man in his teens. As it turned out, she didn't want to marry me. So, I did what young men do. I ran off to join the Marine Corps. It's safe to say that I jumped out of the frying pan and into the fire. With about six months left in the Marine Corps, I took leave and went home to my parents. While at home, I decided to treat my high school wrestling buddy and his wife to dinner. They had been staying at a Christian Drug Rehab house near Stillwater, MN and invited me to join them for a small worship service they were involved in. And that was where I experienced the love of Christ. We shared a good meal and before the night was over I asked my buddy's wife how I could continue to have the love I had experienced during the worship time. And that's when she introduced me to both sin and Jesus.

I learned sin was my problem and that it was ruining my life. I also learned that Jesus could save me from my sin. And just as I didn't know that a slow heart could be the cause of my heart problem, I didn't know sin was the cause of my life problem. Marianne introduced me to Jesus, the only one who could cure my sin problem. That same night, at midnight, in my parent's living room I repented of my sins and believed the Gospel (Mark 1:15; 1 Corinthians 15:3-4; Romans 10:9). Then and there, I began a new life while on leave from the Marine Corps—my sin had been diagnosed, the cure prescribed, and the treatment taken. And it all was at no expense to me! It was by grace through faith, and a gift from God (Ephesians 2:8-9).

And, just as I've become with my heart, I continue to be on high alert because of sin's danger. But sin is not just a danger to me and you—it's mankind's greatest danger. Period.

Sin is the greatest danger to every human on Earth because we all have a sin problem (Romans 3:23). Earth's projected population on January 1, 2023 is 7,942,645,634. Can you imagine the hurt and pain that nearly eight billion defective people can generate?! We're talking about the physical, emotional, and relational breakdown of billions of people. No wonder sin is the greatest danger. Not to mention sinful lifestyle habits can hasten the time of death. Wrong eating, smoking, and drinking ruin our bodies the way salt, poor maintenance, and bad driving habits can ruin a car.

There is nothing good that comes from sin. It ruins everything it touches and inevitably results in death.

What is sin? Sin is not doing what God says to do or doing what Jesus says not to do (James 4:17; Romans 7:7).

The Bible is the written record of what God says to do or not do, to be or not be. Take a look at the Apostle Paul. He became aware he had a sin problem when the Holy Spirit convicted him of coveting. The tenth commandment in Exodus 20:17 states people are not to covet what their neighbor has. What is coveting? Coveting is craving with the intent to get what our neighbor has—his house, wife, male and female servants, ox, donkey, or anything they might own. You and I might not be coveting an ox or a servant, but whatever it might be, if we crave it enough to go after it, we're guilty.

As a non-believer the Apostle Paul tried to stop coveting but found there was nothing he could do on his own to stop. He was a slave to the sin of coveting (Romans 7:14-20). Of course, he wanted to do what was right. The problem was that he simply couldn't on his own. Ultimately, his slavery to sin made him declare what a wretched man he was (Romans 7:24). What is "wretched"? Wretched means that a person is miserable and unhappy. Sin causes us to be miserable and unhappy either now or later. Why later? Because sin may be pleasurable for a period of time, but inevitably it results in misery and unhappiness. Paul was a slave to his sin and was absolutely miserable because of it.

Let's take the example of having a sinful sexual relationship, that is, a sexual relationship outside of marriage. Why is it a sinful relationship? Because the Bible tells us first to be married and then to engage in a sexual relationship with the person we've married for a lifetime. A sexual relationship with no lifetime commitment yields pain for all involved when the pleasure of the act is done and those involved have moved on. STDs, emotional pain, a child without a parent, the possible murder of a child in the womb, and other such things are the result of sexual sin. Sin can also damage sexual relations within a married relationship due to individual sins, such as pornography, an affair, mental and emotional abuse, etc. Without a doubt, sexual sin ultimately makes a person wretched, that is, miserable and unhappy. What's more, all sin eventually leads to unhappiness.

Remember, sin is disobedience to God's instruction in His Word, the Bible, and it causes physical, emotional, and relational breakdown that ends in the death of the physical body. One hundred percent of people sin and die (Romans 3:23; Galatians 5:19-21; Romans 6:23). Why? Because when sin entered the world, it corrupted what was perfect.

Sin Corrupts the Perfect

The Gospel of John introduces us to a man born blind (John 9:1). As they went along, the disciples asked Jesus, "Rabbi, who sinned, this man or his parents that he was born blind?" Jesus answered that neither the man or his parents sinned. He was born blind so that the works of God might be displayed in him (John 9:2-3). Remember, Jesus came to save us from our sins (Matthew 1:21). Keep reading about the blind man in John 9 and you'll see that Jesus not only healed the man's sight but saved this man from the blindness caused by sin right here in the world that had ruined the perfect creation in the beginning.

Before sin entered the world through the disobedience of Adam, no one was born blind (Romans 5:12; Genesis 1:31). Autism, Cystic Fibrosis, poor eyesight, and many such things happen as the result of sin corrupting the world. Destructive weather is because of sin, even when used as a judgment against sin by God, as in the case of Jonah (Jonah 1:1-15). Jonah sinned by running away from the work God wanted him to do. He disobeyed the LORD and the LORD used weather to get him to stop sinning. Guess what? The weather Jonah experienced also affected those not being judged for a specific willful sin.

Defective genes caused by sin entering the world can bring misery to people. The genetic code of a husband and wife can pass an incurable disease such as Cystic Fibrosis to one of their children because sin entered the world and messed with God's perfect creation. My son didn't get Cystic Fibrosis because he sinned. He didn't get Cystic Fibrosis because we, his parents, sinned. Sin corrupted the genetic code of both my wife and me, and together we passed that corruption to our precious son. Sin corrupts all of creation and makes all creation groan in misery (Romans 8:20-23). No matter where we look, sin is the source of all danger and misery.

People infected with sin cause physical, emotional, and relational breakdown and, ultimately, death. Our sin-infected world makes it a hostile place to live for all living creatures. Yet the most dangerous part of sin is the divine judgment it deserves. Yes, sin has caused and will cause death to the physical bodies of all people ever made or born (Genesis 1:27-28; 2:16-17; 3:6; Romans 5:12), but the most dangerous part of sin is the day the person who has sinned is judged by God (Acts 17:30, 31; Hebrews 9:27; Revelation 20:11-15). God will judge each person for his or her sinful thoughts, words, and deeds. The penalty for sin is eternal torment in the Lake of Fire, called the second death. The person who pays the penalty for his sin, that is, the unbeliever who carries his sin with him into death, will suffer in the Lake of Fire for eternity (Revelation 20:15; 21:8; Matthew 25:46). Sin is our greatest danger.

Marianne, my high school friend, helped me see that I was infected by sin and gave me knowledge of the cure for sin. I took the cure that night on the floor of my parents' home when I repented of my sin and believed the gospel. To this day, I'm on high alert for sinful thoughts, speech, and behavior in my life because I know it causes harm to me and all those around me. After all, there is no such thing as sin that affects only the person sinning, even if they're alone on an island. Think about that for a while. Pray on it. Ask and God will give you a greater understanding of our greatest danger—sin.

Consider Your Current Reality

Before moving on to explore what life in a sin-enslaved world looks like, let me ask: have you ever experienced an eye-opening event, such as a heart attack, that caused you to consider either the urgency of the work God has prepared for you in this season of life or the immediate danger of the sin you might be tangled up in? How might your focus, attitude, and faith shift if you were to dive into the assignment God has for you in this season? What might your thought, home, and work-life look like if you were to repent of your sin and turn back to God here and now?

_____

Passages to Reflect On

Galatians 2:20 I have been crucified with Christ. It is no longer I who live, but Christ who lives in me. And the life I now live in the flesh I live by faith in the Son of God, who loved me and gave himself for me. (ESV)

Philippians 4:13 I can do all things through him who strengthens me. (ESV)

Matthew 28:20 teaching them to observe all that I have commanded you.

And behold, I am with you always, to the end of the age." (ESV)

John 14:21 Whoever has my commandments and keeps them, he it is who loves me. And he who loves me will be loved by my Father, and I will love him and manifest myself to him." (ESV)

John 14:23 Jesus answered him, "If anyone loves me, he will keep my word, and my Father will love him, and we will come to him and make our home with him. (ESV)

Mark 1:15 and saying, "The time is fulfilled, and the kingdom of God is at hand; repent and believe in the gospel." (ESV)

1 Corinthians 15:3-4 For I delivered to you as of first importance what I also received: that Christ died for our sins in accordance with the Scriptures, that he was buried, that he was raised on the third day in accordance with the Scriptures, (ESV)

Romans 10:9 because, if you confess with your mouth that Jesus is Lord and believe in your heart that God raised him from the dead, you will be saved. (ESV)

Ephesians 2:8-9 For by grace you have been saved through faith. And this is not your own doing; it is the gift of God, not a result of works, so that no one may boast. (ESV)

Romans 3:23 for all have sinned and fall short of the glory of God, (ESV)

James 4:17 So whoever knows the right thing to do and fails to do it, for him it is sin. (ESV)

Romans 7:7 What then shall we say? That the law is sin? By no means! Yet if it had not been for the law, I would not have known sin. For I would not have known what it is to covet if the law had not said, "You shall not covet." (ESV)

Exodus 20:17 "You shall not covet your neighbor's house; you shall not covet your neighbor's wife, or his male servant, or his female servant, or his ox, or his donkey, or anything that is your neighbor's." (ESV)

Romans 7:14-20 For we know that the law is spiritual, but I am of the flesh, sold under sin. For I do not understand my own actions. For I do not do what I want, but I do the very thing I hate. Now if I do what I do not want, I agree with the law, that it is good. So now it is no longer I who do it, but sin that dwells within me. For I know that nothing good dwells in me, that is, in my flesh. For I have the desire to do what is right, but not the ability to carry it out. For I do not do the good I want, but the evil I do not want is what I keep on doing. Now if I do what I do not want, it is no longer I who do it, but sin that dwells within me. (ESV)

Romans 7:24 Wretched man that I am! Who will deliver me from this body of death? (Rom. 7:24 ESV)

Romans 3:23 for all have sinned and fall short of the glory of God, (ESV)

Galatians 5:19-21 Now the works of the flesh are evident: sexual immorality, impurity, sensuality, idolatry, sorcery, enmity, strife, jealousy, fits of anger, rivalries, dissensions, divisions, envy, drunkenness, orgies, and things like these. I warn you, as I warned you before, that those who do such things will not inherit the kingdom of God. (ESV)

Romans 6:23 For the wages of sin is death, but the free gift of God is eternal life in Christ Jesus our Lord. (ESV)

John 9:1 As he passed by, he saw a man blind from birth. (ESV)

John 9:2-3 And his disciples asked him, "Rabbi, who sinned, this man or his parents, that he was born blind?" Jesus answered, "It was not that this man sinned, or his parents, but that the works of God might be displayed in him. (ESV)

Matthew 1:21 She will bear a son, and you shall call his name Jesus, for he will save his people from their sins." (ESV)

Matthew 5:12 Rejoice and be glad, for your reward is great in heaven, for so they persecuted the prophets who were before you. (ESV)

Genesis 1:31 And God saw everything that he had made, and behold, it was very good. And there was evening and there was morning, the sixth day. (ESV)

Jonah 1:1-15 Now the word of the LORD came to Jonah the son of Amittai, saying, "Arise, go to Nineveh, that great city, and call out against it, for their evil has come up before me." But Jonah rose to flee to Tarshish from the presence of the LORD. He went down to Joppa and found a ship going to Tarshish. So he paid the fare and went down into it, to go with them to Tarshish, away from the presence of the LORD. But the LORD hurled a great wind upon the sea, and there was a mighty tempest on the sea, so that the ship threatened to break up. Then the mariners were afraid, and each cried out to his god. And they hurled the cargo that was in the ship into the sea to lighten it for them. But Jonah had gone down into the inner part of the ship and had lain down and was fast asleep. So the captain came and said to him, "What do you mean, you sleeper? Arise, call out to your god! Perhaps the god will give a thought to us, that we may not perish." And they said to one another, "Come, let us cast lots, that we may know on whose account this evil has come upon us." So they cast lots, and the lot fell on Jonah. Then they said to him, "Tell us on whose account this evil has come upon us. What is your occupation? And where do you come from? What is your country? And of what people are you?" And he said to them, "I am a Hebrew, and I fear the LORD, the God of heaven, who made the sea and the dry land." Then the men were exceedingly afraid and said to him, "What is this that you have done!" For the men knew that he was fleeing from the presence of the LORD, because he had told them. Then they said to him, "What shall we do to you, that the sea may quiet down for us?" For the sea grew more and more tempestuous. He said to them,

"Pick me up and hurl me into the sea; then the sea will quiet down for you, for I know it is because of me that this great tempest has come upon you." Nevertheless, the men rowed hard to get back to dry land, but they could not, for the sea grew more and more tempestuous against them. Therefore they called out to the LORD, "O LORD, let us not perish for this man's life, and lay not on us innocent blood, for you, O LORD, have done as it pleased you." So they picked up Jonah and hurled him into the sea, and the sea ceased from its raging. (ESV)

Romans 8:20-23 For the creation was subjected to futility, not willingly, but because of him who subjected it, in hope that the creation itself will be set free from its bondage to corruption and obtain the freedom of the glory of the children of God. For we know that the whole creation has been groaning together in the pains of childbirth until now. And not only the creation, but we ourselves, who have the firstfruits of the Spirit, groan inwardly as we wait eagerly for adoption as sons, the redemption of our bodies. (ESV)

Genesis 1:27-28 So God created man in his own image, in the image of God he created him; male and female he created them. And God blessed them. And God said to them, "Be fruitful and multiply and fill the earth and subdue it, and have dominion over the fish of the sea and over the birds of the heavens and over every living thing that moves on the earth." (ESV)

Genesis 2:16-17 And the LORD God commanded the man, saying, "You may surely eat of every tree of the garden, but of the tree of the knowledge of good and evil you shall not eat, for in the day that you eat of it you shall surely die." (ESV)

Genesis 3:6 So when the woman saw that the tree was good for food, and that it was a delight to the eyes, and that the tree was to be desired to make one wise, she took of its fruit and ate, and she also gave some to her husband who was with her, and he ate. (ESV)

Romans 5:12 Therefore, just as sin came into the world through one man, and death through sin, and so death spread to all men because all sinned--(ESV)

Acts 17:30-31 The times of ignorance God overlooked, but now he commands all people everywhere to repent, because he has fixed a day on which he will judge the world in righteousness by a man whom he has appointed; and of this he has given assurance to all by raising him from the dead." (17:30 ESV)

Hebrews 9:27 And just as it is appointed for man to die once, and after that comes judgment, (ESV)

Revelation 20:11-15 Then I saw a great white throne and him who was seated on it. From his presence earth and sky fled away, and no place was found for them. And I saw the dead, great and small, standing before the throne, and books were opened. Then another book was opened, which is the book of life. And the dead were judged by what was written in the books, according to what they had done. And the sea gave up the dead who were in it, Death and Hades gave up the dead who were in them, and they were judged, each one of them, according to what they had done. Then Death and Hades were thrown into the lake of fire. This is the second death, the lake of fire. And if anyone's name was not found written in the book of life, he was thrown into the lake of fire. (ESV)

Revelation 20:15 And if anyone's name was not found written in the book of life, he was thrown into the lake of fire. (ESV)

Revelation 21:8 But as for the cowardly, the faithless, the detestable, as for murderers, the sexually immoral, sorcerers, idolaters, and all liars, their portion will be in the lake that burns with fire and sulfur, which is the second death." (ESV)

Matthew 25:46 And these will go away into eternal punishment, but the righteous into eternal life." (ESV)

DIAGNOSE SHIFTING FAITH

CHAPTER 2

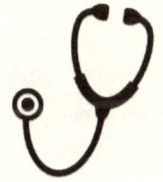

LIFE IN A SIN-ENSLAVED WORLD

Isaiah, the prophet, succinctly states the worldview of a sin-enslaved world.

> Woe to those who call evil good and good evil, who put darkness for
> light and light for darkness, who put bitter for sweet and sweet for
> bitter! (Isaiah 5:20 ESV)

Sin-enslaved? Yes, because most people across the globe are not Christians
according to Jesus (Matthew 7:13-14). And people who are not followers
of Christ are slaves to sin. Jesus even questions if He will find faith on earth
when He comes again (Luke 18:8).

Why do I say that? Paul tells us in Romans 6:16 that if a person is not a
slave to righteousness, they are a slave to sin. Romans 7:15-20 reveals
the frustration of the unbeliever who wants to stop sinning but cannot
because he is held captive as a slave to sin. We know this isn't Paul the
believer, but instead is Paul the unbeliever by what he wrote earlier in his
letter to the Roman Christians—that the believer is no longer a slave to
sin (Romans 6:6). In the Romans 7 passage, the Apostle Paul uses himself
as an example of a person desiring to live according to the Law (God's
instruction) yet has no ability to do so because of indwelling sin. In his
example, Paul called himself a wretched and miserable man who struggled
to stop sinning (Romans 7:24).

Without God, that struggle is futile and filled with obvious traits of deep
brokenness. Revelation 21:4 reveals five things that characterize life in a
sinful world:

- tears

- death

- mourning

- crying

- pain

Have you been touched by any of these five? I know you have because you live alongside me in this sin-infected world. And where there is sin, there is suffering.

The Results of Sin

In the Apostle Paul's letter to the Galatians we get an unsavory taste of what sin causes people to do, both willingly and unwillingly.

> Now the works of the flesh are evident: sexual immorality, impurity, sensuality, idolatry, sorcery, enmity, strife, jealousy, fits of anger, rivalries, dissensions, divisions, envy, drunkenness, orgies, and things like these. I warn you, as I warned you before, that those who do such things will not inherit the kingdom of God. (Galatians 5:19-21 ESV)

In the next few paragraphs we'll touch on how sin impacts our lives.

Let's use the sin of sexual immorality as an example. What is it? What does it look like in real life? It is what caused my sister to hide her pregnancy and deliver twins. It's what caused our family not to see her during the pregnancy or ever to see the twins.

It was around 1967 and as far as I can remember my sister was in her first (and last) year of college. While this was a major event in our family, I personally have no memory of my mom's pain, my sister's pregnancy, or the actual birth of the twins. This type of event unfolds a little differently now in 2023, doesn't it? If a girl gets pregnant outside of marriage, abortion is commonplace. If there is no abortion, the pregnancy is a very public event, whether or not the baby is kept or given up for adoption.

Sexual immorality is common in high school, college, and the workplace and is often accepted or simply overlooked today. A population of eight billion people can generate lots of sin events! Sexual diseases are multiplied. Kids, more often than not, grow up without a father. There is an abundance of tears, death, mourning, crying, and pain caused by the sin of sexual immorality. Think of the tears, death, mourning, crying, and pain caused by sin in individuals, families, schools, communities, states, nations, and the expanse of the world.

The news media report the devastating human and property destruction caused by sin. Countries are invaded, businesses are burned to the ground, gunmen kill multitudes of people, families are breaking apart, and individuals are hooked on alcohol, drugs, gambling, eating disorders, and so on. Can you add to the seemingly endless list of sins we choose to engage in? The cost of our individual and collective sin is enormous, physically, emotionally, and economically.

Add the physical, emotional, and economic toll of weather, heat, drought, and disease, all resulting from sin having entered the world in the beginning, and the cost of sin only multiplies. Do you understand now that sin truly is our greatest danger? Thank God that Jesus came to save us from our sins as well as the original sin that bent the created world into the harsh environment we live in (Matthew 1:21; Romans 8:20, 21).

How about you personally, an individual trekking through this sin-infected world, have you ever shed tears because you were treated harshly or unfairly?

Has the death of a loved one caused you to be angry, lose purpose, and take the joy and peace from your life?

Have you mourned, without comfort, the loss of your health?

Have you cried, frustrated at being misunderstood?

Have you felt the pain of a broken relationship?

These are all the results of sin. And the events surrounding my sister's secret pregnancy all resulted from sin. Worry, fear, harshness, impatience, unkindness, bad habits, addictions, loss of confidence, being unfulfilled, laziness, deceitfulness, etc., are all the overflow of sin into every aspect of our lives! Sin is the greatest danger every person faces in this world. A world enslaved by sin. But guess what? Jesus came to save us from our sins.

The Generational Sin of Romans 1

Our culture in the United States is described by Romans 1:18-32. The events described in this passage have been lived out in every generation since sin entered the world (Genesis 3). The openness of the practice of these sins recorded in Romans 1 waxes and wanes from generation to generation. My parent's generation, my generation, and now my children's and grandchildren's generations have experienced the sins of Romans 1 becoming more public, more domineering, and more accepted in each generation. Let's go through and unpack this a bit.

> For the wrath of God is revealed from heaven against all ungodliness and unrighteousness of men, who by their unrighteousness suppress the truth. For what can be known about God is plain to them, because God has shown it to them. For his invisible attributes, namely, his eternal power and divine nature, have been clearly perceived, ever since the creation of the world, in the things that have been made. So they are without excuse. For although they knew God, they did not honor him as God or give thanks to him, but they became futile in their thinking, and their foolish hearts were darkened. Claiming to be wise, they became fools, and exchanged the glory of the immortal God for images resembling mortal man and birds and animals and creeping things. (Romans 1:18-23 ESV)

Now, consider, for example, how public education began taking God out of the schools back in the 1960s. For instance, God is no longer taught as the Creator as evolution has become the central focus. Evolution teaches that all nature evolved over billions of years without considering the Designer. In the public sphere, God is left out of our children's education.

No God means no acknowledgment of sin, leaving people to do what is right in their own eyes. The Bible is no longer the Truth people live by in our current culture. Instead, truth has become whatever a person believes is truth. Grade school children are now taught there are more than two genders and that gender is not determined by biology but by one's mind and feelings.

The current generation has moved beyond the Truth of the God of the Bible, leaving sin to dictate thinking and behavior. And as people redefine truth to mean whatever they want and believe it to mean, public schools follow suit. A majority of the people in our communities have become futile in their thinking, and their foolish hearts have been darkened and dominated by sin.

> Therefore God gave them up in the lusts of their hearts to impurity, to the dishonoring of their bodies among themselves, because they exchanged the truth about God for a lie and worshiped and served the creature rather than the Creator, who is blessed forever! Amen. (Romans 1:24-25 ESV)

In the 1960s the Hippy movement brought in the sexual revolution. The Biblical norms of a healthy sexual relationship, sheltered in the commitment of marriage between one man and one woman, were beginning to be cast aside. Sex outside of marriage was becoming the social norm. TV shows of the 1950s honored marriage and kept sex mostly between husband and wife, never showing intimate bedroom scenes. The 1960s began to lower the standards to what people wanted. By the 1990s, most sexual relationships portrayed in movies and TV shows were outside of the marriage commitment.

As culture has engaged in lust more and more, TV shows followed suit. And as TV shows entertained with lust, people increasingly gave themselves over to it. It's a vicious cycle, I know. Sinful relationships have become the norm. Isn't this what Paul was describing in his letter to the Romans?

For this reason God gave them up to dishonorable passions. For their women exchanged natural relations for those that are contrary to nature; and the men likewise gave up natural relations with women and were consumed with passion for one another, men committing shameless acts with men and receiving in themselves the due penalty for their error. (Romans 1:26-27 ESV)

We can relate, can't we? Here and now, the sin-enslaved culture of the United States continues to be corrupted more openly and accepted more widely as sin finds a wider audience. Unfortunately, these sinful practices are no longer called sin. Karl Menninger, in his book, *Whatever Happened to Sin,* written in 1978, pointed out this growing change in our cultural attitude toward sinful living. And this is precisely where we are today. If a person calls out an immoral practice as sin, they are said to be expressing hatred. And this sort of upside-down view of sin only picks up steam as sin finds acceptance within a culture.

Sinful sexual expression has become an accepted norm by many people across the country and is a prominent plank in one of two major political parties. What's more, it's regularly being codified into law and even endorsed by the highest social, political, and legal powers in the land. For example, homosexual behavior began to be accepted in the public eye in the 1990s, and by 2015 homosexual marriage was validated by the Supreme Court of the United States of America. In 2023, more and more sinful sexual expression is being normalized, such as transgenderism. Men are now said to be having babies. Of course, biological men can't have babies, yet we're told transgender men can. So it seems even the divine method, language, and experience of pregnancy, like all of God's sexual designs, continue to be corrupted.

That said, it's worth keeping in mind that the same God that sent Jesus to rescue us is also willing to release us to the lustful desires of our hearts and the consequences that follow.

And since they did not see fit to acknowledge God, God gave them up to a debased mind to do what ought not to be done. They were filled with all manner of unrighteousness, evil, covetousness, malice. They are full of envy, murder, strife, deceit, maliciousness. They are gossips, slanderers, haters of God, insolent, haughty, boastful, inventors of evil, disobedient to parents, foolish, faithless, heartless, ruthless. Though they know God's righteous decree that those who practice such things deserve to die, they not only do them but give approval to those who practice them. (Romans 1:28-32 ESV)

We live in this type of sin-enslaved culture, don't you think? Our modern American society is becoming more violent and more evil, and can easily be described by the above scriptures. Consider that the final chapter in history, before the return of Christ, will reveal every Christian being hated, persecuted, jailed, and killed (Matthew 24:9; Revelation 13:10). Why? The end result of a people enslaved by sin is cancel culture to the extreme.

But what about Satan's role in all of this? Satan's power is limited when people put their trust in God. In fact, in James 4:7, we see that when people submit to God and resist the Devil, Satan must flee. Submitting to God means living in obedience to Him while choosing not to practice sin. When we sin, we're doing the work of the Devil (1 John 3:8), but when we obey the Lord Jesus, we resist the Devil causing him to flee. If it isn't clear yet, know that sin is our greatest danger, and Jesus is the only one who can save us from our greatest danger.

In what area of your life do you need to submit to God? How about your habits, actions, beliefs, and attitude? How are you drawing closer to the Lord in this sin-enslaved culture?

The next chapter reveals the key ingredient to how a person can maintain his or her well-being for an abundant life in a sin-enslaved world (Philippians 4:11; John 10:10). But before you move on, spend some time reflecting on the following passages revealed throughout the chapter.

Ask God to open your eyes and ears to His Truth.

Passages to Reflect On

Matthew 7:13-14 "Enter by the narrow gate. For the gate is wide and the way is easy that leads to destruction, and those who enter by it are many. For the gate is narrow and the way is hard that leads to life, and those who find it are few. (ESV)

Luke 18:8 I tell you, he will give justice to them speedily. Nevertheless, when the Son of Man comes, will he find faith on earth?" (ESV)

Romans 6:16 Do you not know that if you present yourselves to anyone as obedient slaves, you are slaves of the one whom you obey, either of sin, which leads to death, or of obedience, which leads to righteousness? (ESV)

Romans 7:15-20 For I do not understand my own actions. For I do not do what I want, but I do the very thing I hate. Now if I do what I do not want, I agree with the law, that it is good. So now it is no longer I who do it, but sin that dwells within me. For I know that nothing good dwells in me, that is, in my flesh. For I have the desire to do what is right, but not the ability to carry it out. For I do not do the good I want, but the evil I do not want is what I keep on doing. Now if I do what I do not want, it is no longer I who do it, but sin that dwells within me. (ESV)

Romans 6:6 We know that our old self was crucified with him in order that the body of sin might be brought to nothing, so that we would no longer be enslaved to sin. (ESV)

Romans 7:24 Wretched man that I am! Who will deliver me from this body of death? (ESV)

Revelation 21:4 He will wipe away every tear from their eyes, and death shall be no more, neither shall there be mourning, nor crying, nor pain anymore, for the former things have passed away." (ESV)

Matthew 1:21 She will bear a son, and you shall call his name Jesus, for he will save his people from their sins." (ESV)

Romans 8:20-21 For the creation was subjected to futility, not willingly, but because of him who subjected it, in hope that the creation itself will be set free from its bondage to corruption and obtain the freedom of the glory of the children of God. (ESV)

Matthew 24:9 "Then they will deliver you up to tribulation and put you to death, and you will be hated by all nations for my name's sake. (ESV)

Revelation 13:10 If anyone is to be taken captive, to captivity he goes; if anyone is to be slain with the sword, with the sword must he be slain. Here is a call for the endurance and faith of the saints. (ESV)

James 4:7 Submit yourselves therefore to God. Resist the devil, and he will flee from you. (ESV)

1 John 3:8 Whoever makes a practice of sinning is of the devil, for the devil has been sinning from the beginning. The reason the Son of God appeared was to destroy the works of the devil. (ESV)

Philippians 4:11 Not that I am speaking of being in need, for I have learned in whatever situation I am to be content. (ESV)

John 10:10 The thief comes only to steal and kill and destroy. I came that they may have life and have it abundantly. (ESV)

CHAPTER 3

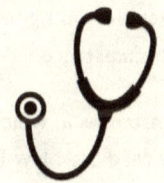

LIVING VICTORIOUS
IN A
SIN-ENSLAVED
WORLD

Living with a constant sense of well-being requires a lot of help, especially considering we live in a sin-corrupted world with 8 billion fellow sin-infected people. As we dig in, I want to point out that well-being is not the absence of tears, mourning, crying, or pain. On the contrary, we have and experience *well-being* despite simultaneously experiencing the effects of sin.

Think about it like this: here in Wisconsin I live in a harsh climate. In particular, the winters are incredibly cold. However, I have the resources to keep my home comfortable even on the coldest days, making it possible for me to live in this hostile climate and still have a sense of well-being. In this chapter we're going to unpack the God-given resources that assure the believer's well-being in any circumstance.

That said, let's look at the circumstances in which the Apostle Paul experienced well-being. If you've read the New Testament you know his circumstances weren't always on the up and up. Knowing that the followers of Jesus would struggle in their walk, he personally divulges a number of harsh life experiences in his second letter to the Church in Corinth in order to encourage us (2 Corinthians 1:3-10; 4:7-12; 6:3-10; 7:4; 11:23-31). We're also told of his trials in the book of Acts and how the Lord helped him. (Acts 13:50-52; 14:4-7, 19-20; 16:16-40; 27:39-28:6, 16-31). We see that despite these trials, Paul's own testimony in his letter to the Philippians reveals that he learned to be content (experience a sense of well-being) in all circumstances (Philippians 4:11-12).

And it isn't just that Paul was able to experience contentment, it's the way he lived content in all circumstances, revealed in his letter to the Galatian Christians (Galatians 2:20) and also in his second letter to the Corinthian Church (2 Corinthians 5:7) that ought to catch our attention.

Affliction and Contentment

Paul experienced affliction in Asia that was beyond his strength. He felt he would be put to death, yet was content in this circumstance by relying on God. The very God who raises the dead.

Paul was afflicted in every way—but not crushed,

he was perplexed—but not driven to despair,

he was persecuted—but not forsaken,

he was struck down—but not destroyed.

How would your well-being hold up if you were in Paul's shoes, experiencing the circumstances just described?

Paul, by his own testimony, was content. He experienced hardships, calamities, beatings, imprisonments, riots, troubles, sleepless nights, hunger, dishonor, slander, treatment as an imposter, discipline from God, sorrow, and poverty—but he remained content. Five times he received thirty-nine lashes with a whip for preaching the Gospel. He was beaten with rods three times. He was even shipwrecked three times. Once, he was stoned. If that wasn't enough, he was in danger from rivers, robbers, his own people, the Gentiles, in the city, in the wilderness, at sea, and from false brothers. Whew! Can you imagine experiencing even a fraction of those trials? Or do you know anyone who has and, by God's grace, managed to remain content through it all?

Did I mention that Paul was often without food and without sleep as well? That he was often cold and exposed to inclement weather. Yet he testified to his contentment in all circumstances! The question is, how did he maintain his sense of well-being through all of this? How can I? How can you? How can any believer in Jesus experience contentment through even a fraction of these trials?

The Key to Contentment

Paul clued us into his source of contentment by declaring that he did all things through Christ who strengthened him (Philippians 4:13), that he lived by faith in the Son of God (Galatians 2:20), and that he lived by faith, not by sight (2 Corinthians 5:7). His key declaration underpinning his divine contentment is unpacked in Galatians 2:20. This verse is the Apostle Paul's testimony of how he lived the Christian life with a sense of well-being in all circumstances. Let's spend some time unpacking Paul's key to contentment.

"The life I live in the flesh (physical body), I live by faith in the Son of God."

First and foremost, Paul's faith was in Jesus Christ, the Son of God. Faith, which can be translated as *trust* or *belief* throughout the Scriptures, is central to experiencing contentment here in the flesh. For Paul, it's the starting point for what follows. The question is, why did Paul put his trust in the Son of God in the first place? His answer is simple, Jesus was crucified on the cross and raised from the dead on the third day just as He said would happen (Luke 9:21-23; 24:6-9, 36-49; 1 Corinthians 15:3-11, 20). It's easy to understand how he could trust someone who is able to conquer death, don't you think?

With God's help Paul obeyed the first two commands of Jesus, "Repent and believe the gospel." Gospel means *good news*. And repent, in the context Jesus used it, means to turn away from sin and toward Jesus for eternal pardon from sin. True repentance is revealed in us first by a desire to change the way we live and second by fulfilling that desire with lifestyle changes.

What's more, when Paul repented and believed the Gospel, he received the promised Holy Spirit (Ephesians 1:13-14). Every person who repents of their sin and believes the Gospel receives the promised Holy Spirit. When we receive the Holy Spirit, two incredible things happen:

1. The person who receives the Holy Spirit is guaranteed eternal life (Ephesians 1:14).

2. The person who receives the Holy Spirit receives all the resources of God needed to live a victorious life in a sin-enslaved world.

When we repent and believe the Gospel, like Paul, we can say that we "have been crucified with Christ" completely and forever. Period. When Christ was crucified on the cross, He fulfilled the curse of the Law, which is death, and overcame the power of sin and Satan (Romans 5:10; 6:6-7; Hebrew 2:14-15). The person crucified with Christ is pardoned from the death penalty and has become a victor over sin, our greatest danger, and over Satan, our enemy (Ephesians 6:12; James 4:7). The person who believes the Gospel—that Jesus died on the cross for our sins, was raised from the dead on the third day, and that Jesus is Lord—has received the capacity to live in victory over sin, now and forever (1 Corinthians 15:3-4; Romans 10:9).

Praising God yet?

Paul goes on.

"It is no longer I who live, but Christ who lives in me."

That's an awesome claim, isn't it? In fact, every true believer has God living inside of them. Romans 8:9-11 makes it very clear—God is living in the true believer. On the other hand, it also makes clear that if a person does not have the Spirit of Christ (God), they are not a believer.

Paul wrote in Ephesians 1:13 that every person who repents of his sin and believes the Gospel receives the promised Holy Spirit. Why the adjective "promised?" Ezekiel, the prophet, spoke God's Word to his people when he said, "And I will put my Spirit within you, and cause you to walk in my statutes and be careful to obey my rules" (Ezekiel 36:27). That very promise made through Ezekiel was fulfilled after Jesus ascended back into heaven and sent the Holy Spirit to be in everyone who believes the Gospel. After all, the Holy Spirit is referred to as "the promised Holy Spirit."

God keeps his promises, doesn't he (2 Corinthians 1:20)? Every believer has every resource necessary to obey God's Word, the Bible, which means that you and I can be and do everything God's word says we are to be and do. This also means that we can refrain from being and doing what God's word forbids. Since Christ lives in us, we have every spiritual blessing in the heavenlies, all the fruit of the Spirit, all the strength we need, the hope we need, and every single one of the Lord's promises. Did I mention we have all the riches of Christ inside of us (Ephesians 1:3; Galatians 5:22-23; Ephesians 1:18-20; 3:20; 1 Peter 1:3; 2 Peter 1:3-4)?

As believers, we are fully capable of maintaining a sense of well-being in any circumstance. Remember, *well-being* is not freedom from tears, death of loved ones, mourning over losses, crying, and pain—*well-being* is what sustains the believer experiencing the result of a sin-enslaved world. The believer in Jesus is not only a victor in the end but is equipped to live as a victor in all the circumstances life presents in this sin-enslaved world, right here and right now.

If you haven't already, read the passages referenced at the beginning of the chapter. In fact, be sure to read and reflect on all the scriptures mentioned throughout and written in full at the end of the chapter in order to gain a clearer sense of how pain and well-being can be experienced at the same time in the life of a follower of Jesus.

Connecting the Dots

So far, I've presented every believer in Jesus as a victor, not a victim. And believers, as a result of Jesus living inside of them, have access to His resources—ultimately, the living God. Since everything a believer has is given by God, neither people nor Satan can take from them what God has given. As it stands, the believer has the capacity to live with a sense of well-being in any circumstance. Now, he or she can run the race of life as *victor*, not simply to *achieve victory*. As eternal victors, believers are seated in the heavenlies (Ephesians 2:6) and living life as more than conquerors in Christ (Romans 8:37). The key to all the resources a victorious believer has in Christ is faith in the Son of God.

When Paul said, "The life I live in the flesh, I live by faith in the Son of God," he was revealing the key to God-designed well-being as victors in Christ. "How do I get this key?" you ask. You already have it, and you already used it to enter into eternal life (Ephesians 2:8-9). The key is faith in the Son of God. After all, faith is a gift from God. A gift He gave in order to pardon us from the penalty of sin. A gift given to us when we received the Holy Spirit upon believing the Gospel.

Every believer has faith in the Son of God, Jesus. So every believer has a key. Since we know how to get this key (by faith), the next question to ask is, "How does the believer use the key of faith to access all the resources of Christ inside of them?"

Paul's prayer in 2 Thessalonians 1:11 gives us great insight into how to use the faith we have been gifted—how to use the key to experience a sense of well-being in any circumstance.

> To this end *we always pray* for you, *that our God* may make you worthy of his calling and *may fulfill* every resolve for good and *every work of faith by his power*... (2 Thessalonians 1:11 ESV)

Paul, on behalf of the Thessalonian believers, asked the Lord to fulfill every work of their faith by His power. You see, the believers were to begin or attempt to do the work God had given them to do while trusting God to fulfill their attempt by his power. In faith, they set out on mission, and by faith, they trusted God to empower them to act. That's it, the definition of the key of faith: *faith attempts to be or do God's will, expecting Him to fulfill our attempts with His power*.

This short book, for example, is written by faith in the Son of God. When I look at my own abilities, I don't see a writer. Yet, by faith, I'm attempting to write this freeing truth, expecting the Lord to fulfill my attempt at writing with his power. Which means that, if you're reading this chapter, you're a witness to the fact that the Lord helped me do what was impossible for me to do on my own. And you know what? You can trust that He'll do the same for you. After all, we're already living as victors, right? And the key to this victorious life is to live 24/7 by faith in Jesus alone.

With that victorious life in mind, take a moment and assess where your current source of well-being lies. Do you feel victorious when your faith is in a relationship, a local church, a happy event, or even a prized possession? Or do you find that your faith in Christ is the source of your confidence in this broken world? When was the last time you honestly contemplated the reality that the power of the Living God is at work in your life?

After reflecting on the following passages, dig into the next chapter and discover what a believer's life is meant to be while living in this sin-enslaved world.

Passages to Reflect On

Philippians 4:11-12 Not that I am speaking of being in need, for I have learned in whatever situation I am to be content. I know how to be brought low, and I know how to abound. In any and every circumstance, I have learned the secret of facing plenty and hunger, abundance and need. (ESV)

2 Corinthians 1:3-10 Blessed be the God and Father of our Lord Jesus Christ, the Father of mercies and God of all comfort, who comforts us in all our affliction, so that we may be able to comfort those who are in any affliction, with the comfort with which we ourselves are comforted by God. For as we share abundantly in Christ's sufferings, so through

Christ we share abundantly in comfort too. If we are afflicted, it is for your comfort and salvation; and if we are comforted, it is for your comfort, which you experience when you patiently endure the same sufferings that we suffer. Our hope for you is unshaken, for we know that as you share in our sufferings, you will also share in our comfort. For we do not want you to be unaware, brothers, of the affliction we experienced in Asia. For we were so utterly burdened beyond our strength that we despaired of life itself. Indeed, we felt that we had received the sentence of death. But that was to make us rely not on ourselves but on God who raises the dead. He delivered us from such a deadly peril, and he will deliver us. On him we have set our hope that he will deliver us again. (ESV)

2 Corinthians 4:7-12 But we have this treasure in jars of clay, to show that the surpassing power belongs to God and not to us. We are afflicted in every way, but not crushed; perplexed, but not driven to despair; persecuted, but not forsaken; struck down, but not destroyed; always carrying in the body the death of Jesus, so that the life of Jesus may also be manifested in our bodies. For we who live are always being given over to death for Jesus' sake, so that the life of Jesus also may be manifested in our mortal flesh. So death is at work in us, but life in you. (ESV)

2 Corinthians 6:3-10 We put no obstacle in anyone's way, so that no fault may be found with our ministry, but as servants of God we commend ourselves in every way: by great endurance, in afflictions, hardships, calamities, beatings, imprisonments, riots, labors, sleepless nights, hunger; by purity, knowledge, patience, kindness, the Holy Spirit, genuine love; by truthful speech, and the power of God; with the weapons of righteousness for the right hand and for the left; through honor and dishonor, through slander and praise. We are treated as impostors, and yet are true; as unknown, and yet well known; as dying, and behold, we live; as punished, and yet not killed; as sorrowful, yet always rejoicing; as poor, yet making many rich; as having nothing, yet possessing everything. (ESV)

2 Corinthians 7:4 I am acting with great boldness toward you; I have great pride in you; I am filled with comfort. In all our affliction, I am overflowing with joy. (ESV)

2 Corinthians 11:23-31 Are they servants of Christ? I am a better one-- I am talking like a madman-- with far greater labors, far more imprisonments, with countless beatings, and often near death. Five times I received at the hands of the Jews the forty lashes less one. Three times I was beaten with rods. Once I was stoned. Three times I was shipwrecked; a night and a day I was adrift at sea; on frequent journeys, in danger from rivers, danger from robbers, danger from my own people, danger from Gentiles, danger in the city, danger in the wilderness, danger at sea, danger from false brothers; in toil and hardship, through many a sleepless night, in hunger and thirst, often without food, in cold and exposure. And, apart from other things, there is the daily pressure on me of my anxiety for all the churches. Who is weak, and I am not weak? Who is made to fall, and I am not indignant? If I must boast, I will boast of the things that show my weakness. The God and Father of the Lord Jesus, he who is blessed forever, knows that I am not lying. (ESV)

Acts 13:50-52 But the Jews incited the devout women of high standing and the leading men of the city, stirred up persecution against Paul and Barnabas, and drove them out of their district. But they shook off the dust from their feet against them and went to Iconium. And the disciples were filled with joy and with the Holy Spirit. (ESV)

Acts 14:4-7 But the people of the city were divided; some sided with the Jews and some with the apostles. When an attempt was made by both Gentiles and Jews, with their rulers, to mistreat them and to stone them, they learned of it and fled to Lystra and Derbe, cities of Lycaonia, and to the surrounding country, and there they continued to preach the gospel. (ESV)

Acts 14:19-20 But Jews came from Antioch and Iconium, and having persuaded the crowds, they stoned Paul and dragged him out of the city, supposing that he was dead. But when the disciples gathered about him, he rose up and entered the city, and on the next day he went on with Barnabas to Derbe. (ESV)

Acts 16:16-40 As we were going to the place of prayer, we were met by a slave girl who had a spirit of divination and brought her owners much gain by fortune-telling. She followed Paul and us, crying out, "These men are servants of the Most High God, who proclaim to you the way of salvation." And this she kept doing for many days. Paul, having become greatly annoyed, turned and said to the spirit, "I command you in the name of Jesus Christ to come out of her." And it came out that very hour. But when her owners saw that their hope of gain was gone, they seized Paul and Silas and dragged them into the marketplace before the rulers. And when they had brought them to the magistrates, they said, "These men are Jews, and they are disturbing our city. They advocate customs that are not lawful for us as Romans to accept or practice." The crowd joined in attacking them, and the magistrates tore the garments off them and gave orders to beat them with rods. And when they had inflicted many blows upon them, they threw them into prison, ordering the jailer to keep them safely. Having received this order, he put them into the inner prison and fastened their feet in the stocks. About midnight Paul and Silas were praying and singing hymns to God, and the prisoners were listening to them, and suddenly there was a great earthquake, so that the foundations of the prison were shaken. And immediately all the doors were opened, and everyone's bonds were unfastened. When the jailer woke and saw that the prison doors were open, he drew his sword and was about to kill himself, supposing that the prisoners had escaped. But Paul cried with a loud voice, "Do not harm yourself, for we are all here." And the jailer called for lights and rushed in, and trembling with fear he fell down before Paul and Silas. Then he brought them out and said, "Sirs, what must I do to be saved?" And they said, "Believe in the Lord Jesus, and you will be saved, you and your household." And they spoke the word of the Lord to him and to all who were in his house. And he took them the same hour of the night and washed their wounds; and he was baptized at once, he and all his family. Then he brought them up into his house and set food before them. And he rejoiced along with his entire household that he had believed in God. But when it was day, the magistrates sent the police, saying, "Let those men go." And the jailer reported these words to Paul, saying, "The magistrates have sent to let you go. Therefore come out now and go in peace." But Paul said to them, "They have beaten us publicly, uncondemned, men who are Roman citizens, and have thrown us into prison; and do they now throw us out secretly? No! Let them come themselves and take us out." The police reported these words to the magistrates, and they were afraid when they heard that they were Roman citizens. So they came and apologized to them. And they took them out and asked them to leave the city. So they went out of the prison and visited Lydia. And when they had seen the brothers, they encouraged them and departed. (ESV)

Acts 27:39-44 Now when it was day, they did not recognize the land, but they noticed a bay with a beach, on which they planned if possible to run the ship ashore. So they cast off the anchors and left them in the sea, at the same time loosening the ropes that tied the rudders. Then hoisting the foresail to the wind they made for the beach. But striking a reef, they ran the vessel aground. The bow stuck and remained immovable, and the stern was being broken up by the surf. The soldiers' plan was to kill the prisoners, lest any should swim away and escape. But the centurion, wishing to save Paul, kept them from carrying out their plan. He ordered those who could swim to jump overboard first and make for the land, and the rest on planks or on pieces of the ship. And so it was that all were brought safely to land. (ESV)

28:1-6 After we were brought safely through, we then learned that the island was called Malta. The native people showed us unusual kindness, for they kindled a fire and welcomed us all, because it had begun to rain and was cold. When Paul had gathered a bundle of sticks and put them on the fire, a viper came out because of the heat and fastened on his hand. When the native people saw the creature hanging from his hand, they said to one another, "No doubt this man is a murderer. Though he has escaped from the sea, Justice has not allowed him to live." He, however, shook off the creature into the fire and suffered no harm. They were waiting for him to swell up or suddenly fall down dead. But when they had waited a long time and saw no misfortune come to him, they changed their minds and said that he was a god. (ESV)

Acts 27:16-31 Running under the lee of a small island called Cauda, we managed with difficulty to secure the ship's boat. After hoisting it up, they used supports to undergird the ship. Then, fearing that they would run aground on the Syrtis, they lowered the gear, and thus they were driven along. Since we were violently storm-tossed, they began the next day to jettison the cargo. And on the third day they threw the ship's tackle overboard with their own hands. When neither sun nor stars appeared for many days, and no small tempest lay on us, all hope of our being saved was at last abandoned. Since they had been without food for a long time, Paul stood up among them and said, "Men, you should have listened to me and not have set sail from Crete and incurred this injury and loss. Yet now I urge you to take heart, for there will be no loss of life among you, but only of the ship. For this very night there stood before me an angel of the God to whom I belong and whom I worship, and he said, 'Do not be afraid, Paul; you must stand before Caesar. And behold, God has granted you all those who sail with you.' So take heart, men, for I have faith in God that it will be exactly as I have been told. But we must run aground on some island." When the fourteenth night had come, as we were being driven across the Adriatic Sea, about midnight the sailors suspected that they were nearing land. So they took a sounding and found twenty fathoms. A little farther on they took a sounding again and found fifteen fathoms. And fearing that we might run on the rocks, they let down four anchors from the stern and prayed for day to come. And as the sailors were seeking to escape from the ship, and had lowered the ship's boat into the sea under pretense of laying out anchors from the bow, Paul said to the centurion and the soldiers, "Unless these men stay in the ship, you cannot be saved." (ESV)

Galatians 2:20 I have been crucified with Christ. It is no longer I who live, but Christ who lives in me. And the life I now live in the flesh I live by faith in the Son of God, who loved me and gave himself for me. (ESV)

2 Corinthians 5:7 for we walk by faith, not by sight. (ESV)

Philippians 4:13 I can do all things through him who strengthens me. (ESV)

Galatians 2:20 I have been crucified with Christ. It is no longer I who live, but Christ who lives in me. And the life I now live in the flesh I live by faith in the Son of God, who loved me and gave himself for me. (ESV)

2 Corinthians 5:7 for we walk by faith, not by sight. (ESV)

Luke 9:21-23 And he strictly charged and commanded them to tell this to no one, saying, "The Son of Man must suffer many things and be rejected by the elders and chief priests and scribes, and be killed, and on the third day be raised." And he said to all, "If anyone would come after me, let him deny himself and take up his cross daily and follow me. (ESV)

Luke 24:6-9 He is not here, but has risen. Remember how he told you, while he was still in Galilee, that the Son of Man must be delivered into the hands of sinful men and be crucified and on the third day rise." And they remembered his words, and returning from the tomb they told all these things to the eleven and to all the rest. (ESV)

Luke 24:36-49 As they were talking about these things, Jesus himself stood among them, and said to them, "Peace to you!" But they were startled and frightened and thought they saw a spirit. And he said to them, "Why are you troubled, and why do doubts arise in your hearts? See my hands and my feet, that it is I myself. Touch me, and see. For a spirit does not have flesh and bones as you see that I have." And when he had said this, he showed them his hands and his feet. And while they still disbelieved for joy and were marveling, he said to them, "Have you anything here to eat?" They gave him a piece of broiled fish, and he took it and ate before them. Then he said to them, "These are my words that I spoke to you while I was still with you, that everything written about me in the Law of Moses and the Prophets and the Psalms must be fulfilled." Then he opened their minds to understand the Scriptures, and said to them, "Thus it is written, that the Christ should suffer and on the third day rise from the dead, and that repentance and forgiveness of sins should be proclaimed in his name to all nations, beginning from Jerusalem. You are witnesses of these things. And behold, I am sending the promise of my Father upon you. But stay in the city until you are clothed with power from on high." (ESV)

1 Corinthians 15:3-11 For I delivered to you as of first importance what I also received: that Christ died for our sins in accordance with the Scriptures, that he was buried, that he was raised on the third day in accordance with the Scriptures, and that he appeared to Cephas, then to the twelve. Then he appeared to more than five hundred brothers at one time, most of whom are still alive, though some have fallen asleep. Then he appeared to James, then to all the apostles. Last of all, as to one untimely born, he appeared also to me. For I am the least of the apostles, unworthy to be called an apostle, because I persecuted the church of God. But by the grace of God I am what I am, and his grace toward me was not in vain. On the contrary, I worked harder than any of them, though it was not I, but the grace of God that is with me. Whether then it was I or they, so we preach and so you believed. (ESV)

1 Corinthians 15:20 But in fact Christ has been raised from the dead, the firstfruits of those who have fallen asleep. (ESV)

Ephesians 1:13-14 In him you also, when you heard the word of truth, the gospel of your salvation, and believed in him, were sealed with the promised Holy Spirit, who is the guarantee of our inheritance until we acquire possession of it, to the praise of his glory. (ESV)

Ephesians 1:4 even as he chose us in him before the foundation of the world, that we should be holy and blameless before him. In love (ESV)

Romans 5:10 For if while we were enemies we were reconciled to God by the death of his Son, much more, now that we are reconciled, shall we be saved by his life. (ESV)

Romans 6:6-7 We know that our old self was crucified with him in order that the body of sin might be brought to nothing, so that we would no longer be enslaved to sin. For one who has died has been set free from sin. (ESV)

Hebrews 2:14-15 Since therefore the children share in flesh and blood, he himself likewise partook of the same things, that through death he might destroy the one who has the power of death, that is, the devil, and deliver all those who through fear of death were subject to lifelong slavery. (ESV)

Ephesians 6:12 For we do not wrestle against flesh and blood, but against the rulers, against the authorities, against the cosmic powers over this present darkness, against the spiritual forces of evil in the heavenly places. (ESV)

James 4:7 Submit yourselves therefore to God. Resist the devil, and he will flee from you. (ESV)

1 Corinthians 15:3-4 For I delivered to you as of first importance what I also received: that Christ died for our sins in accordance with the Scriptures, that he was buried, that he was raised on the third day in accordance with the Scriptures, (ESV)

Romans 10:9 because, if you confess with your mouth that Jesus is Lord and believe in your heart that God raised him from the dead, you will be saved. (ESV)

Romans 8:9-11 You, however, are not in the flesh but in the Spirit, if in fact the Spirit of God dwells in you. Anyone who does not have the Spirit of Christ does not belong to him. But if Christ is in you, although the body is dead because of sin, the Spirit is life because of righteousness. If the Spirit of him who raised Jesus from the dead dwells in you, he who raised Christ Jesus from the dead will also give life to your mortal bodies through his Spirit who dwells in you. (ESV)

Ezekiel 36:27 And I will put my Spirit within you, and cause you to walk in my statutes and be careful to obey my rules. (ESV)

2 Corinthians 1:20 For all the promises of God find their Yes in him. That is why it is through him that we utter our Amen to God for his glory. (ESV)

Ephesians 1:3 Blessed be the God and Father of our Lord Jesus Christ, who has blessed us in Christ with every spiritual blessing in the heavenly places, (ESV)

Galatians 5:22-23 But the fruit of the Spirit is love, joy, peace, patience, kindness, goodness, faithfulness, gentleness, self-control; against such things there is no law. (ESV)

Ephesians 1:18-20 having the eyes of your hearts enlightened, that you may know what is the hope to which he has called you, what are the riches of his glorious inheritance in the saints, and what is the immeasurable greatness of his power toward us who believe, according to the working of his great might that he worked in Christ when he raised him from the dead and seated him at his right hand in the heavenly places, (ESV)

I Peter 1:3 Blessed be the God and Father of our Lord Jesus Christ! According to his great mercy, he has caused us to be born again to a living hope through the resurrection of Jesus Christ from the dead, (ESV)

2 Peter 1:3-4 His divine power has granted to us all things that pertain to life and godliness, through the knowledge of him who called us to his own glory and excellence, by which he has granted to us his precious and very great promises, so that through them you may become partakers of the divine nature, having escaped from the corruption that is in the world because of sinful desire. (ESV)

Ephesians 2:6 and raised us up with him and seated us with him in the heavenly places in Christ Jesus, (ESV)

Romans 8:37 No, in all these things we are more than conquerors through him who loved us. (ESV)

Ephesians 2:8-9 For by grace you have been saved through faith. And this is not your own doing; it is the gift of God, not a result of works, so that no one may boast. (ESV)

CHAPTER 4

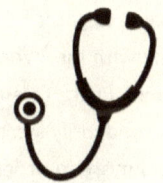

WHAT A BELIEVER'S LIFE IS MEANT TO BE

When I call my doctor with a health problem I expect him to give me an educated opinion concerning my health. Why? Because I know that he's spent years learning in medical school and training in the field about the physical body and how it's expected to function. I assume he knows how a healthy body works, that he can tell me how I've become unhealthy, and what I need to do to get back to good health.

You've been to a doctor's office, right? So you know this process. After checking in, the nurse first gets my weight and height, takes my blood pressure and temperature, and finally asks what medicines I'm on and what supplements I'm taking. Their goal is to gather current health data to help my doctor diagnose what's wrong with me. When my doctor comes into the exam room, he reviews the initial data, listens to my heart and lungs, then begins to ask me questions to identify symptoms of ill health. He may take x-rays, order blood tests, and more in order to understand where my body has departed from good health.

After diagnosis, he prescribes a treatment best suited to address my symptoms and helps me to recover back to good health. In fact, no diagnosis is possible, and no treatment can be prescribed if the doctor does not know the standard of good health or the ways to restore it in the first place.

So, let's connect that process to my spiritual life. If I don't know the standard of a godly life in Christ, then I don't have the ability to diagnose an ungodly life in Christ. Suppose I don't know how to become godly, maintain godliness, and be restored to godliness. In that case, I can't prescribe what to do to restore a person suffering from a spiritual illness (ungodliness). Over the next few pages, we're going to spend time describing what spiritual health looks like. In later chapters, we'll cover the diagnosis, ways to restore good spiritual health, and how to maintain good spiritual health in any circumstance. For now, let's look at what it means to live a healthy spiritual life.

Paul's Example

The Apostle Paul wrote fourteen letters to churches at various stages of their spiritual growth in order to reveal good spiritual health, diagnose spiritual illness, and even prescribe how to return to and maintain good spiritual health when they veered off track (2 Timothy 3:16). How was he able to write with confidence? Because Paul knew what good spiritual health looked like, how to diagnose ill health, what was needed to return to godliness, and what it looked like to live out a godly life.

If you've read Paul's letters then you know that he was an eager student of the written Word throughout his life (2 Timothy 3:16-17; 2 Timothy 4:13). He grew up studying the Scriptures (Old Testament) and, as a follower of Christ, received revelation from Jesus along the way (Galatians 1:12). But he was also a man of prayer. Prayer is conversation between a believer and the Lord. Speaking with and listening to Jesus. Over time, Paul became an expert in teaching, rebuking, correcting, and training in righteousness by regularly meeting with the Lord in the Word and in prayer.

We can do the same thing and, in fact, are commanded in Philippians 4:9 to follow Paul's example, "What you have learned and received and heard and seen in me—*practice* these things, and the God of peace will be with you." Catch that? You and I, believers in Jesus, are capable of being confident in the Word and consistent in prayer in order to know and live healthy Christian lives.

Spiritually Healthy Living

From the time my kids were young, I've daily practiced Deuteronomy 6:4-7. Why? Because I wanted my children to experience the abundant and eternal life Jesus came to give to all who repent of their sins and believe the Gospel. In today's language, "well-being in any circumstance now and forever" describes the abundant life I wanted for my kids and now desire for my grandkids. Our Lord intends for us to experience the fullness of the resources He gave us the moment we believed the Gospel and received the Holy Spirit. And what we were given reveals what God meant for a believer's life to look like in a sin-enslaved world.

Let's look at several passages that foster this idea of what we have been given for our well-being.

In John's Gospel, Jesus said, "The thief comes only to steal and kill and destroy. I came that they may have life and have it abundantly" (John 10:10). How incredible that Jesus, the Creator God, tells each one of us that He came to give us eternal and abundant life. How do I know "have life" includes both eternal and temporal life?

I know it by John 3:16, "For God so loved the world, that he gave his only Son, that whoever believes in him should not perish but have *eternal life*."

I know it by John 16:33, "I have said these things to you, that in me you may have peace. In the world you will have tribulation. But take heart; I have overcome the world."

The life Jesus has equipped us to live is abundant both now and forever. In this sin-enslaved world we experience tears, death, mourning, crying, and pain, but we also experience a sense of well-being. This is something that only a believer in Jesus can experience simultaneously. He also told us to rejoice and be glad when we are reviled, persecuted, and accused falsely of doing evil on account of following Him (Matthew 5:11, 12). Why? Because Jesus told us we would have peace in Him while we are experiencing tribulation in the world.

As Paul testified in 2 Corinthians 7:4, "I am acting with great boldness toward you; I have great pride in you; I am filled with comfort. *In all our affliction, I am overflowing with joy.*" And again in Philippians 4:11, "Not that I am speaking of being in need, *for I have learned in whatever situation I am to be content.*" See that? Believers are equipped by God to live paradoxical lives in this sin-enslaved world. To be clear, I'm using *abundant, contentment,* and *well-being* synonymously, and this God-defined sense of well-being is achieved by using all the resources the Lord has given to His followers.

Our God-given Resources

The Apostle Paul revealed in Galatians 5:22-23 what is ours, or what we have in Christ, because the Holy Spirit lives in us. You're probably familiar with this list but read it through again. Take your time.

> But the fruit of the Spirit is love, joy, peace, patience, kindness, goodness, faithfulness, gentleness, self-control; against such things there is no law.

When we first repented of our sins and believed the Gospel, we received the Holy Spirit (Ephesians 1:13). If a person does not have the Holy Spirit, that person is not a believer and therefore is not saved from his or her sins (Romans 8:9-11). Since every believer has the Holy Spirit, every single believer has access to all the spiritual fruit in any and every circumstance. The nine qualities of the fruit of the Spirit are not resident at all times within just anyone. Only the believer in Jesus is resourced with and has access to the fruit of the Spirit.

People, groups, events, and possessions, no matter how important or impactful they might be, are not the source of the fruit and cannot take the fruit from us. The Holy Spirit is the only 24/7 source of the fruit. It is ours to experience in all circumstances, all the time. What does this mean? It means that believers have the capacity to live this paradox in faith. We can mourn the death of a loved one and still have a sense of well-being. We can be in the most intolerable situation and still have a sense of well-being. Why? Our love, joy, peace, patience, kindness, goodness, faithfulness, gentleness, and self-control depend only on the Holy Spirit. Nothing can prevent Him from manifesting the fruit in our lives to give us a sense of well-being, that is, nothing but our refusal to access it God's way. He has given us the key to access all we need in order to live with a sense of well-being. In the previous chapter we learned how to access God's resources in order to be content in any circumstance. Remember what it was?

"The life I live in the flesh (body), I live by faith in the Son of God" (Galatians 2:20c).

Christians are equipped by God with hope, the riches of His glorious inheritance, and immeasurably great power. Paul specifically prays in Ephesians 1:16-20 that we would experientially know all three. "I do not cease to give thanks for you, *remembering you in my prayers,* that the God of our Lord Jesus Christ, the Father of glory, may give you a spirit of wisdom and of revelation in the knowledge of him, having the eyes of your hearts enlightened, *that you may know what is the hope* to which he has called you, *what are the riches of his glorious inheritance* in the saints, and *what is the immeasurable greatness of his power* toward us who believe, according to the working of his great might that he worked in Christ when he raised him from the dead and seated him at his right hand in the heavenly places."

The hope Paul expresses is a living hope—the risen Christ. Not even death could conquer Him.

The hope is a certain hope—nothing can hinder it. Philippians 1:6 states the certainty of God getting His work done in us. "And I am sure of this, that he who began a good work in you will bring it to completion at the day of Jesus Christ."

Now consider the wealth we have inherited as you read the following passages:

> In him we have *redemption through his blood, the forgiveness of our trespasses,* according to the riches of his grace… (Ephesians 1:7)

> …so that in the coming ages he might show *the immeasurable riches of*

his grace in kindness toward us in Christ Jesus. (Ephesians 2:7)

...to me, though I am the very least of all the saints, *this grace was given, to preach* to the Gentiles *the unsearchable riches of Christ*... (Ephesians 3:8)

...that according to *the riches of his glory* he may grant you *to be strengthened with power through his Spirit in your inner being*... (Ephesians 3:16)

And my God will *supply every need of yours* according to *his riches in glory in Christ Jesus.* (Philippians 4:19)

We have been given power beyond measure to experience well-being in any circumstance. That's an incredible cause and effect, isn't it? God's power within us equals well-being within us. No tears, death, mourning, crying, or pain can stomp out our hope, exhaust our riches, or overcome our power to go on in life with a sense of well-being.

Brothers and sisters in Christ, we are equipped with every spiritual blessing in the heavens (Ephesians 1:3). How often do you sit back and reflect on these in prayer, in celebration, or during a season of struggle? And what are they? These spiritual blessings are Jesus' joy and peace and every other spiritual benefit in the heavens received by the believer. The Greek word translated blessing refers to a *favor* or *benefit* bestowed by God. We have every spiritual benefit that exists in God's dwelling place. We can experience the spiritual benefits of heaven at the same time we are experiencing the emotional and physical disadvantages of our sin-enslaved world.

The Apostle Peter reveals the total package of benefits that we have received as believers of the Gospel. In 2 Peter 1:3-4 he says, "His divine power has granted to us all things that pertain to life and godliness, through the knowledge of him who called us to his own glory and excellence, by which he has granted to us his precious and very great promises, so that through them you may become partakers of the divine nature, having escaped from the corruption that is in the world because of sinful desire."

The Greek grammar makes it clear we have everything we need to partake in His divine nature in any season or circumstance we find ourselves in. And be sure to keep in mind that our resources include all the promises of God, and He keeps all His promises (2 Corinthians 1:20).

Our Lord meant for us to experience the well-being of His dwelling place in heaven here and now while we experience the corruption that is in the world caused by sinful desires. The corruption causes us to experience tears, death, mourning, and pain while having a sense of well-being because of all God has given us in Christ. These spiritual resources are what allow us to recognize what it means to live a healthy Christian life as well as diagnose the symptoms of spiritually unhealthy habits, attitudes, practices, and beliefs. And we access all His resources by faith in the Son of God, that is, Jesus, the Creator God. Jesus experienced on earth everything we will experience in this life, and He lived victoriously through it with a sense of well-being, showing us the way. But He also experienced on the cross something we will never share as believers, the penalty of death. Now He lives in us to empower us to be content in every circumstance.

The next four chapters will help us diagnose when our faith has shifted away from Christ and onto a person, group, event, or possession. Before you read on, spend some time reflecting on the Scripture all throughout this chapter. When was the last time you assessed your daily walk with Christ? Are you healthy? How about your family? Spend some time praying that God would open your eyes more and more to healthy Christlike living as well as any symptoms of waning faith.

Passages to Reflect On

2 Timothy 3:16 All Scripture is breathed out by God and profitable for teaching, for reproof, for correction, and for training in righteousness, (ESV)

Galatians 1:12 For I did not receive it from any man, nor was I taught it, but I received it through a revelation of Jesus Christ. (ESV)

2 Timothy 3:16-17 All Scripture is breathed out by God and profitable for teaching, for reproof, for correction, and for training in righteousness, that the man of God may be complete, equipped for every good work. (ESV)

2 Timothy 4:13 When you come, bring the cloak that I left with Carpus at Troas, also the books, and above all the parchments. (ESV)

Deuteronomy 6:4-7 "Hear, O Israel: The LORD our God, the LORD is one. You shall love the LORD your God with all your heart and with all your soul and with all your might. And these words that I command you today shall be on your heart. You shall teach them diligently to your children, and shall talk of them when you sit in your house, and when you walk by the way, and when you lie down, and when you rise. (ESV)

Matthew 5:11-12 "Blessed are you when others revile you and persecute you and utter all kinds of evil against you falsely on my account. Rejoice and be glad, for your reward is great in heaven, for so they persecuted the prophets who were before you. (ESV)

Galatians 5:22-23 But the fruit of the Spirit is love, joy, peace, patience, kindness, goodness, faithfulness, gentleness, self-control; against such things there is no law. (ESV)

Ephesians 1:13 In him you also, when you heard the word of truth, the gospel of your salvation, and believed in him, were sealed with the promised Holy Spirit, (ESV)

Romans 8:9-11 You, however, are not in the flesh but in the Spirit, if in fact the Spirit of God dwells in you. Anyone who does not have the Spirit of Christ does not belong to him. But if Christ is in you, although the body is dead because of sin, the Spirit is life because of righteousness. If the Spirit of him who raised Jesus from the dead dwells in you, he who raised Christ Jesus from the dead will also give life to your mortal bodies through his Spirit who dwells in you. (ESV)

Ephesians 1:3 Blessed be the God and Father of our Lord Jesus Christ, who has blessed us in Christ with every spiritual blessing in the heavenly places, (ESV)

2 Corinthians 1:20 For all the promises of God find their Yes in him. That is why it is through him that we utter our Amen to God for his glory. (ESV)

CHAPTER 5

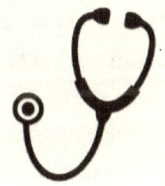

DIAGNOSING THE SHIFT FROM GOD TO A PERSON

"I'm dead but alive." This is how I described myself when, as I mentioned in chapter one, I found out the girl I wanted to marry didn't want to marry me. But that was before I became a believer in Jesus Christ. After all, those are not the words of a person experiencing a sense of well-being, are they? It was on the heels of that personal declaration that I ran off to join the Marine Corps.

Why did I lose my sense of well-being and run away? Well, the person I had trusted to provide my happiness and fulfillment no longer wanted to provide those for me. The person I trusted to give me purpose no longer wanted or needed me. Maybe you can relate. I trusted in someone that did not have the capacity to give me the happiness, fulfillment, and purpose I needed to be content. The reality is that no person can always be our source of well-being in every circumstance. In fact, no created being whatsoever can do that—only Jesus has such capacity.

And when, with only six months left in the Marine Corps, I was introduced to Jesus, repented of my sins, and believed the Gospel, I entered into a relationship with the only One who could ultimately fulfill my life in any circumstance.

You see, when we put our trust in a person in a misguided attempt to provide for the entirety of our well-being, the opposite will inevitably happen—we will not have a constant sense of well-being. As believers in Jesus Christ, our Lord and Savior, we can have a constant sense of well-being in any situation, but only if our faith is in God alone. Exercising faith in God alone means we're living in obedience to His will.

How can I say that? What does salvation have to do with obedience?

Saving faith has within it the element of obedience. In fact, in Romans 1:5 and 16:26, Paul taught that saving faith yields obedience. When we come to believe the Gospel, we're believing in the death, resurrection, and *lordship* of Jesus (1 Corinthians 15:3-4; Romans 10:9). And when we believe the Gospel, we receive the promised Holy Spirit and thus not only the desire to obey but also the ability to obey. The Holy Spirit was promised in Ezekiel 36:27 and given to anyone who repents of his or her sin and believes the Gospel (Ephesians 1:13). As believers filled with the Holy Spirit, we obey by exercising faith in Jesus. By faith, they're attempting to obey and expecting God to fulfill their attempt with His power (Galatians 2:20; 2 Thessalonians 1:11).

On the other hand, when we don't obey the Word of God, we are not exercising faith in Jesus alone. Why? Because if we claim that Jesus is Lord yet don't submit to His Truth, then we simply aren't placing our faith in Him. And that sort of off-the-mark faith leads to all the pain the world has to offer.

Let's take some time and explore a few examples that reveal a faith that has shifted from God to a person. After that, we'll take a look at the damaging effects of trusting in a person for well-being and not in God alone—the damaging effects both on the person *trusting* and the person *being trusted*.

Shifting Faith

Someone who relies on the sinful world believes they need the right environment relationally, the right physical health, the right job, the right material provision, and the right community to have a sense of well-being. But what happens if the person we are trusting in doesn't have the ability to generate the right emotions within us?

Or give us good health?

Or help us develop meaningful relationships?

Or help us pursue our interests in the workplace?

Or actively and successfully participate in our community the way we desire?

Societal well-being may very well desert us, leaving us isolated by sickness, old age, or the responsibility to care for a disabled family member if the person we're placing our faith in can't fulfill our desire to thrive in the community around us. There are a lot of ifs and false expectations when we depend upon our own ability or the ability of another human for our sense of well-being, aren't there? The good news is that Jesus has the ability to give us a sense of well-being when we or another person have no ability to provide the right environment, opportunities, or help we need to do what supports our sense of well-being.

Take your time as you read through the following examples that reveal symptoms that enable us to diagnose the problem when our faith has shifted to a person instead of God alone.

Irritation

One seemingly universal symptom that our faith is shifting to a person, a symptom we've all displayed, is getting irritated at the individual we've put our trust in. Irritation with someone is an indication that our faith rests on the one we've grown irritated with, that they've failed to do or say what gives us a sense of well-being. And you know what? These people are, more often than not, family members.

Let's say you had a long, hard day at work and are really looking forward to a good meal and a relaxing evening at home. Once home, however, your two sons, close in age, begin to argue, accusing one another. Of course, you're tired, and so you tell them to settle down and be quiet. But they're boys in the middle of an argument. They don't listen to you. What do you do? You raise your voice. You yell at them. Unfortunately, that doesn't solve anything and they keep on fighting with one another.

What's going on here? Simply put, you've grown irritated with them and seek to shut them up because you want to relax. Do you know what that

DIAGNOSE SHIFTING FAITH

means? It means your faith was in your kids to behave in such a way that you could relax, and they failed to speak or behave in the manner you wanted. Instead of obeying the Lord and gently restoring your sinful kids (Galatians 6:1), you got irritated with them, yelling in order to get what you desired. Your faith shifted from Jesus alone to your kids—kids who have no ability to give you a constant sense of well-being.

Irritation is a standout symptom of our faith having shifted from God alone to a person. Think about many of the things that irritate you. How many of them are the result of misplaced trust and false expectations? At the end of the day, irritation is a sin since it is not obeying the Bible. "Where does it say that?" you ask. In Proverbs 12:16, the author says that "The vexation of a fool is known at once, but the prudent ignores an insult." Vexation means *irritation* or *annoyance*. The Bible tells us we are to live as wise people. Fools get irritated, not the wise. Fools sin, not the wise. Irritation is a sin. When we sin, we are not living by faith in God alone.

Who have you been getting irritated with lately?

Worry

Trusting a person to fulfill our physical needs, then worrying about that provision is another symptom of a shifting faith. Nowhere in the Scriptures are we instructed to trust a person for our physical needs. Yes, people are instructed to provide for the physical needs of those they are responsible for, but they are not told to trust others to meet their physical needs.

We may not even know we're trusting in someone to meet our physical needs until they move away, pass away, or are simply unable to provide for us. When we no longer have the provision they supplied, we grow anxious and begin to worry about how our needs will be met. Worry reveals our faith shifted to a person and was not in God alone. Worry, like irritation, is sin. After all, the Bible tells us not to worry (Philippians 4:6). Only God is able to provide for us physically in any circumstance. He alone promises that if we seek first His kingdom and righteousness, He will provide (Matthew 6:11, 25-34).

As it stands, the Lord will provide all we need to do His will in any circumstance or environment. We can properly diagnose when our faith has shifted to a person when we begin to worry about how our physical and financial needs will be met when that person can't provide.

What worries have begun to crowd out your faith lately?

Fear

Another symptom that our faith has shifted is fear of what a person may say or do to cause us harm. In the Bible, fear is contrasted with faith in God (Proverbs 29:25). So, when we begin to fear what another person says about us or what his or her actions might do to harm us, we lose our sense of well-being. Maybe we're afraid they might cause us to lose our job or our reputation or cause social and personal persecution. But if we trust our job and our reputation to God alone, then no matter what happens, our well-being is secure and enjoyed.

In this case, fear is the symptom that leads us to diagnose that our faith has shifted from God alone to a person. When we recognize fear is at work in our life, we can repent of our shifting faith, confess it as sin, and ask the Lord to help us get our faith back in Him alone. We begin to ask God to not only remove our fear but also remind us daily of His power at work within us to overcome that fear.

There are many symptoms that reveal our faith has shifted to a person, too many to list here (see the appendix for a more extensive list). Recognizing symptoms, just as we do with an illness, is how we diagnose that our faith has shifted from God alone to a person. Irritation, worry, and fear are sins; if we're in sin, we're not exercising faith in the One and Only Jesus. However, when we do exercise faith in God alone, we obey His Word, the Bible.

Irritation, misplaced trust, and fear are symptoms that can help us to diagnose a shifted faith. The people we grow irritated with, worry about losing, or fear have become the objects of our trust. When we trust a person for fulfillment, peace, or safety, we're in sin because the Bible instructs us to trust God alone to meet our needs, whether physical, emotional, relational, or spiritual.

Remember, the Lord has never instructed us to trust a person for our well-being. If we trust in the Lord alone for our well-being, then we can truly love even our enemies, we can respond in love to a person who sins by gently restoring him, and we can keep our well-being when a person's words or actions could cause us harm.

The Negative Effects of an Intermittent Faith

So, what are some of the negative effects of a shifting faith? Here's the deal, when we trust a person for our well-being, we're setting ourselves up for disappointment at best and devastation and hopelessness at worst.

Most of us live with an intermittent sense of well-being. When a person we trust benefits us, we have a sense of well-being, so we're happy, cheerful, generous, and kind. We feel all is going our way.

However, when the person we trust disappoints or wounds us, we lose our sense of well-being and become self-protective, sad, mad, or unkind. We feel like everything is against us.

We escape the intermittent sense of well-being by:

1. Quickly diagnosing that our faith has shifted to a person.

2. Repenting, that is, turning away from our sin and toward God.

3. Confessing our sin of trusting a person for our well-being and the evil fruit of irritation, etc.

And finally, asking God for help in placing our trust back in Him alone.

Did you ever consider that the people we entrust our well-being to also experience negative effects? They aren't being treated as *they'd* like to be. Why? They were put in a position to fail, unable to meet the needs of the person trusting them, and so causing turmoil simply because they couldn't provide what only God can. This is a cold and unsettling environment to be in. A person in this position sometimes wonders what they might have done wrong to hurt, irritate, or anger the one trusting them, and often with no opportunity to inquire, converse, or even explain himself freely.

When we trust a person instead of God alone, we tend to damage our relationship with the person and with the Lord. As followers of Christ, we don't have to give in to the despair of misplaced trust. We don't have to walk around like the living dead, but if we find ourselves in this position, even intermittently, it's important for us to be able to quickly diagnose it and shift our faith back to God alone.

So, let's learn to act more quickly. What has irritated you recently? Why? Can you diagnose where your faith shifted to?

How about worry—what has worried you in recent days, weeks, or months? Are you trusting a person and not God alone?

Or fear—what's causing you to be afraid lately? If you were to give a reason for your fear, what would it be? And how might specifically naming your fear help you diagnose where your faith has shifted to?

Spend some time reflecting on the following passages, asking God to help you discern where your faith is and what you can do to place it back on Him.

Passages to Reflect On

Romans 1:5 through whom we have received grace and apostleship to bring about the obedience of faith for the sake of his name among all the nations, (ESV)

Romans 16:26 but has now been disclosed and through the prophetic writings has been made known to all nations, according to the command of the eternal God, to bring about the obedience of faith-- (ESV)

1 Corinthians 15:3-4 For I delivered to you as of first importance what I also received: that Christ died for our sins in accordance with the Scriptures, that he was buried, that he was raised on the third day in accordance with the Scriptures, (ESV)

Romans 10:9 because, if you confess with your mouth that Jesus is Lord and believe in your heart that God raised him from the dead, you will be saved. (ESV)

Ezekiel 36:27 And I will put my Spirit within you, and cause you to walk in my statutes and be careful to obey my rules. (ESV)

Ephesians 1:13 In him you also, when you heard the word of truth, the gospel of your salvation, and believed in him, were sealed with the promised Holy Spirit, (ESV)

Galatians 2:20 I have been crucified with Christ. It is no longer I who live, but Christ who lives in me. And the life I now live in the flesh I live by faith in the Son of God, who loved me and gave himself for me. (ESV)

2 Thessalonians 1:11 To this end we always pray for you, that our God may make you worthy of his calling and may fulfill every resolve for good and every work of faith by his power, (ESV)

Galatians 6:1 Brothers, if anyone is caught in any transgression, you who are spiritual should restore him in a spirit of gentleness. Keep watch on yourself, lest you too be tempted. (ESV)

Matthew 6:11 Give us this day our daily bread, (ESV)

Matthew 6:25-34 "Therefore I tell you, do not be anxious about your life, what you will eat or what you will drink, nor about your body, what you will put on. Is not life more than food, and the body more than clothing? Look at the birds of the air: they neither sow nor reap nor gather into barns, and yet your heavenly Father feeds them. Are you not of more value than they? And which of you by being anxious can add a single hour to his span of life? And why are you anxious about clothing? Consider the lilies of the field, how they grow: they neither toil nor spin, yet I tell you, even Solomon in all his glory was not arrayed like one of these. But if God so clothes the grass of the field, which today is alive and tomorrow is thrown into the oven, will he not much more clothe you, O you of little faith? Therefore do not be anxious, saying, 'What shall we eat?' or 'What shall we drink?' or 'What shall we wear?' For the Gentiles seek after all these things, and your heavenly Father knows that you need them all. But seek first the kingdom of God and his righteousness, and all these things will be added to you. "Therefore do not be anxious about tomorrow, for tomorrow will be anxious for itself. Sufficient for the day is its own trouble. (ESV)

Proverbs 29:25 The fear of man lays a snare, but whoever trusts in the LORD is safe. (ESV)

CHAPTER 6

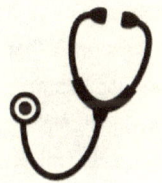

DIAGNOSING THE SHIFT FROM GOD TO A GROUP

In the last chapter we focused on diagnosing a shift in our faith when it moves from God to a person. Now, let's take that same diagnostic practice and expand it from trusting in a person for our well-being to trusting in a group. Think of some of the groups in our communities, cities, and nation that people might trust for their well-being.

People trust in the government, the local church, their place of employment, clubs, political parties, teams, social groups, etc.

There are any number of groups we might place our trust in, aren't there? No doubt you managed to think of one or two to add to the list. But what does it mean to put our trust in a group? What does it look like? What happens when we do? In the following examples, we'll touch on a few of the more common groups an individual might place their faith in. And, like we did when attempting to diagnose our misplaced faith in people, we'll attempt to learn how to recognize the symptoms of a shifting faith in God alone toward groups.

Government

"How exactly do I put my trust in the government?" you ask. Well, let me ask a few questions the way a doctor might in search of the underlying issue. After all, recognizing the symptoms will help us know we are trusting the government for our well-being instead of Creator God.

Does it affect your well-being if the government violates your trust? Remember that well-being is rooted in our faith-filled contentment in the abundance of Jesus, who is in us and resourcing us with all we need. In light of that Christ-centered definition, let me ask again—if the government violates your trust, is your well-being turned upside down?

Listen, we trust the government for safety. We also trust our police force for local protection from wrong. And we rely on our national military for protection from enemy governments. Now, God said He would use these organizations to protect us from the wrong-doer (Romans 13:1-5). And if they're a moral police force or military, we trust them to do their job and to do it well. However, no matter how good they might be, we aren't supposed to trust them for our overall well-being. You see, we trust these protection groups to do their job, but we trust God alone to keep us safe.

Consider, if the military is defeated and our nation was conquered by another nation, as Christians we would still have our well-being because we trust God alone for our safety. Yes, we are told by God to prepare our military for battle, but in the same breath, we're told to trust God alone for victory (Proverbs 21:31).

Or how about this, in retirement we trust the government to send our Social Security check on time. We trust the government to do what the law says regarding our monetary resources—but even so, we're called to trust in God alone for our financial provision (Matthew 6:25, 33).

Here's the deal, we know that our faith has shifted to the government when the government begins to make laws contrary to the Bible, causing us to worry about our safety. Why? Because God is greater than our government and provides for our well-being even when the government fails to do its job. Remember, it's a sin to worry (Philippians 4:6). When we worry, we know our faith is not in God alone. If our faith truly was in God alone, we would say, "No!" to worry. Our faith in God would compel us to present what worries us to God with thanksgiving, trusting Him to guard our hearts and minds with His peace that passes understanding (Philippians 4:6-7).

We diagnose our faith has shifted to the government when we exhibit the symptom of worry if and when the government goes against our Biblical beliefs.

With that in mind, how would you diagnose your faith regarding the government? What worries you? What do you do with that worry when it rises up in your heart and mind?

RAY HAAS

65

Employer

We trust our employer to hold up their end of the bargain, don't we? We believe they will provide the agreed-upon pay for our work. However, just as it is with individuals and governments, God never intended us to trust our employers for our material needs (Matthew 6:25, 33; Philippian 4:19). God alone orchestrates the meeting of our needs and shifting that trust, or reliance, onto our employer to meet our needs is sin.

Take a moment and make it personal. Suppose you get laid off from work and begin to worry about how you're going to provide for your family. Maybe you've been in this position. Keep in mind that worry is a symptom of our faith having shifted from God to our employer. We know that God deeply cares about our material needs and the needs of our families. Yet when we worry, we're assuming not only that He doesn't care but also that He isn't in control.

And, just as it is with shifting faith in other areas of life, when we recognize the symptom of worry, we can diagnose that our faith has shifted from God alone to our employer. Only then can we prayerfully and faithfully seek God to help us fully rely on Him.

Local Church

Do people trust their local church for their well-being? It can happen. And it almost sounds appropriate, doesn't it? After all, the local church is a united body of believers. The body of Christ. It's good to trust the local church!

How does a believer shift from trusting God to trusting in the local church? Picture this. A believer loves to go to church and hear a message from the Lord. He goes to be built up in love. And he even finds joy in serving within his gifted area. One day, however, he gets a job promotion, moves to a different city, and begins to look for a local church to attend. But there's a problem. No local church is like the Body he left behind. The sermons by the pastor are not as good, no one is building him up like he used to experience at his old church, and he hasn't found a place to serve. After a short period he longs for their old church, is dissatisfied, and ultimately has no sense of well-being.

That person's lack of contentment with his church experience is a symptom that his faith was in his former local church and not God alone.

Connecting the Dots

As believers, we're equipped to be content in any situation, but can only use the resources Jesus has given for our contentment by faith in God alone (Philippians 4:11; Galatians 2:20). If we begin to trust our local church to provide for our well-being, we dam up the resources and blessings we need and that God provides for our sense of well-being. You see, when the believer trusts in God alone for everything, God will send the grace they need by the people He has gifted and sent (Hebrews 4:16; 1 Peter 4:10; 1 Corinthians 12:4-11). God responds to our faith in Him by helping us use the blessings and resources He has given us in Christ (Ephesians 1:3; Galatians 5:22-23; 2 Peter 1:3-4).

We're provided groups by our Lord to enhance our lives. Yet even the most profoundly faithful groups are made up of sinful people that do not have the capacity to provide for what we need 100% of the time for us to experience a totally fulfilling sense of well-being or contentment. Groups will fail us in the same way that individual people fail us.

Take some time and consider the groups, big and small, in person and online, inside and outside of the Church, that you have been putting your trust in. Do you recognize any of the symptoms of shifting faith? Remember, God will never fail us or forsake us. On the contrary, He is always available to help us (Hebrews 13:5-6). As you reflect on the source of your faith, be sure to meditate on the Scriptures throughout this chapter. Ask God to reveal Himself more and more as the singularly reliable source of your faith.

Passages to Reflect On

Romans 13:1-5 Let every person be subject to the governing authorities. For there is no authority except from God, and those that exist have been instituted by God. Therefore whoever resists the authorities resists what God has appointed, and those who resist will incur judgment. For rulers are not a terror to good conduct, but to bad. Would you have no fear of the one who is in authority? Then do what is good, and you will receive his approval, for he is God's servant for your good. But if you do wrong, be afraid, for he does not bear the sword in vain. For he is the servant of God, an avenger who carries out God's wrath on the wrongdoer. Therefore one must be in subjection, not only to avoid God's wrath but also for the sake of conscience. (ESV)

Proverbs 21:31 The horse is made ready for the day of battle, but the victory belongs to the LORD. (ESV)

Matthew 6:25, 33 "Therefore I tell you, do not be anxious about your life, what you will eat or what you will drink, nor about your body, what you will put on. Is not life more than food, and the body more than clothing?... 33But seek first the kingdom of God and his righteousness, and all these things will be added to you. (ESV)

Philippians 4:6 do not be anxious about anything, but in everything by prayer and supplication with thanksgiving let your requests be made known to God. (ESV)

Philippians 4:6-7 do not be anxious about anything, but in everything by prayer and supplication with thanksgiving let your requests be made known to God. And the peace of God, which surpasses all understanding, will guard your hearts and your minds in Christ Jesus. (ESV)

Philippians 4:19 And my God will supply every need of yours according to his riches in glory in Christ Jesus. (ESV)

Philippians 4:11 Not that I am speaking of being in need, for I have learned in whatever situation I am to be content. (ESV)

Galatians 2:20 I have been crucified with Christ. It is no longer I who live, but Christ who lives in me. And the life I now live in the flesh I live by faith in the Son of God, who loved me and gave himself for me. (ESV)

Hebrews 4:16 Let us then with confidence draw near to the throne of grace, that we may receive mercy and find grace to help in time of need. (ESV)

1 Peter 4:10 As each has received a gift, use it to serve one another, as good stewards of God's varied grace: (ESV)

1 Corinthians 12:4-11 Now there are varieties of gifts, but the same Spirit; and there are varieties of service, but the same Lord; and there are varieties of activities, but it is the same God who empowers them all in everyone. To each is given the manifestation of the Spirit for the common good. For to one is given through the Spirit the utterance of wisdom, and to another the utterance of knowledge according to the same Spirit, to another faith by the same Spirit, to another gifts of healing by the one Spirit, to another the working of miracles, to another prophecy, to another the ability to distinguish between spirits, to another various kinds of tongues, to another the interpretation of tongues. All these are empowered by one and the same Spirit, who apportions to each one individually as he wills. (ESV)

Ephesians 1:3 Blessed be the God and Father of our Lord Jesus Christ, who has blessed us in Christ with every spiritual blessing in the heavenly places, (ESV)

Galatians 5:22-23 But the fruit of the Spirit is love, joy, peace, patience, kindness, goodness, faithfulness, gentleness, self-control; against such things there is no law. (ESV)

2 Peter 1:3-4 His divine power has granted to us all things that pertain to life and godliness, through the knowledge of him who called us to his own glory and excellence, by which he has granted to us his precious and very great promises, so that through them you may become partakers of the divine nature, having escaped from the corruption that is in the world because of sinful desire. (ESV)

Hebrews 13:5-6 Keep your life free from love of money, and be content with what you have, for he has said, "I will never leave you nor forsake you." So we can confidently say, "The Lord is my helper; I will not fear; what can man do to me?" (ESV)

CHAPTER 7

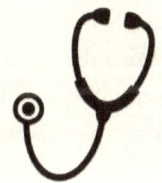

DIAGNOSING THE SHIFT FROM GOD TO AN EVENT

We may not think events can shake our deepest sense of well-being, but they can. It is very possible for a single event to cause us to shift our faith away from God. Just consider a few rather normal events, big and small, that can cause a shift. Imagine a birthday goes by unnoticed. Might that cause us to feel unloved? Or what about the loss of a job? Or how do we respond when the vacation gets canceled? And would we still be content on a fixed income, even as inflation erodes it? In these momentary events, are we content or unsettled? Do we fall into sin by complaining and casting blame on someone? Do we succumb to worry?

No doubt you can think of any number of events, some mundane while others life-altering, that might cause a shift in faith. Yet throughout each one, we have the opportunity to maintain a faith centered on God alone and, where we fall short, recognize the symptoms of our shifting faith and turn back to Christ. That said, let's work through a few examples, some common events that often foster a shift in our faith.

Celebrations

Some people don't like to celebrate their birthdays. You probably know someone like this. It might even be you. After all, it's just another day, right? But some people would be heartbroken if their birthday wasn't recognized. If they weren't greeted in the morning with a vibrant "Happy Birthday!" or even mildly doted on throughout the day. To them, a birthday is an important event leaned on in order to sustain their well-being or to simply feel loved.

While annual family celebrations, such as birthdays, are opportunities for experiencing and expressing love, what do you suppose are some symptoms that can help us recognize that our faith might have shifted to the event rather than being totally in Jesus?

Loss of joy is one. Self-doubt could be another.

"Aren't I important to people?"

"Doesn't anybody love me?"

When our joy, identity, and worthiness to be loved are lost because an event such as a birthday celebration didn't happen, it's clear that we've put our faith in the event and not solely in the Lord. When we get angry because our birthday party was forgotten, we're in sin (James 1:20; Romans 12:17; 1 Peter 3:9). And sin robs us of the joy we have in knowing that the Lord never forgets us. It robs us of the gratefulness we have for His gift of life and faith.

Job Loss

As we noted in the last chapter, one of the groups in our life that can cause a faith-shift revolves around our employment. Related to that is the unfortunate event of losing our job. On the one hand, this can be a learning experience when our faith is in God alone. However, while I'm by no means making light of the impact that losing a job has on our life, it's a symptom of a shifting faith if it shakes our contentment, abundant life, or, said another way, our well-being—all the more if we begin to call ourselves a failure in light of our loss.

I remember feeling like a failure when I lasted only two years at the first church I served. My faith had shifted to the event of being a successful pastor. After the fact, once I returned to trusting in the Lord alone, I could see the experience so clearly, including all that I had learned in those two years and all that I still needed to learn. Rather than wallow in feeling like a failure, I went back to school, completed my master's degree, and went on to start a local mission-sending church. The short-term event of my early pastoral experience shifted from a focus on the so-called failure back to God and the lessons only He could teach through faith.

If I haven't yet been clear on this, our well-being is not dependent on a temporal event.

We're prone to have a sense of well-being if an event succeeds but quickly lose our sense of well-being if an event fails. If our faith is in God alone, we may very well be disappointed if an event doesn't meet our standard of success, but our well-being remains intact. We can seek God, evaluate, and move on as a more experienced person. Ultimately, we leave the results in God's hands. After all, He alone is before, within, and beyond all the events, good and bad, that we'll ever experience. It only makes sense that faith in Him alone is the proper response to the diagnosis of a faith that's shifted.

Connecting the Dots

If we begin to worry about provision when we lose our job, it's a symptom that our faith has shifted to the event of our job rather than remaining in God alone. After all, it's God who promised to provide what we need, one day at a time, so long as we seek first His kingdom and righteousness (Matthew 6:25-34).

And for those of us on a fixed income in retirement, the event of inflation can rob us of our sense of well-being if we are trusting in the strength of the economy to provide our income. On the other hand, when we trust in the strength of the Lord, we'll experience contentment despite a faltering economy, fully aware that the Lord will keep His promise to provide for us. Worrying about the economy is a symptom of a shifted faith.

Trusting the results of an event for our success, even an event that's important to us is a symptom of a shifted faith. We are to trust God for our success, not the results of an event (Genesis 24:12; Nehemiah 1:11; Proverbs 21:31; Luke 9:21-22). Likewise, suppose we find ourselves scrambling to get to a church service to experience worship, relieve our loneliness, or fill our spiritual tank. In that case, we should know this is a symptom of shifted faith. Trusting a sporting event, a concert, marriage, social get-togethers, our work, a vacation, or even a date night to fulfill our deepest pleasure is a symptom of faith that has shifted.

We can trust the Lord to provide all that we need and yes, that includes our pleasure (1 Timothy 6:17). So, let's take some time and reflect on events that have in the past and are currently impacting our faith and state of well-being. What events have caused you a loss of contentment, and do you know how to recover the loss? Are you gaining the ability to diagnose when your faith has shifted from God alone to a person, group, or event?

Psalm 112:7 offers wise counsel, "He is not afraid of bad news; his heart is firm, *trusting in the LORD*." If we take this to heart, no doubt it will support our well-being and help us keep from sinning no matter how adverse an event in our life might prove to be.

Passages to Reflect On

James 1:20 for the anger of man does not produce the righteousness of God. (ESV)

Romans 12:17 Repay no one evil for evil, but give thought to do what is honorable in the sight of all. (ESV)

1 Peter 3:9 Do not repay evil for evil or reviling for reviling, but on the contrary, bless, for to this you were called, that you may obtain a blessing. (ESV)

Matthew 6:25-34 "Therefore I tell you, do not be anxious about your life, what you will eat or what you will drink, nor about your body, what you will put on. Is not life more than food, and the body more than clothing? Look at the birds of the air: they neither sow nor reap nor gather into barns, and yet your heavenly Father feeds them. Are you not of more value than they? And which of you by being anxious can add a single hour to his span of life? And why are you anxious about clothing? Consider the lilies of the field, how they grow: they neither toil nor spin, yet I tell you, even Solomon in all his glory was not arrayed like one of these. But if God so clothes the grass of the field, which today is alive and tomorrow is thrown into the oven, will he not much more clothe you, O you of little faith? Therefore do not be anxious, saying, 'What shall we eat?' or 'What shall we drink?' or 'What shall we wear?' For the Gentiles seek after all these things, and your heavenly Father knows that you need them all. But seek first the kingdom of God and his righteousness, and all these things will be added to you. "Therefore do not be anxious about tomorrow, for tomorrow will be anxious for itself. Sufficient for the day is its own trouble. (ESV)

Genesis 24:12 And he said, "O LORD, God of my master Abraham, please grant me success today and show steadfast love to my master Abraham. (ESV)

Nehemiah 1:11 O Lord, let your ear be attentive to the prayer of your servant, and to the prayer of your servants who delight to fear your name, and give success to your servant today, and grant him mercy in the sight of this man." Now I was cupbearer to the king. (ESV)

Proverbs 21:31 The horse is made ready for the day of battle, but the victory belongs to the LORD. (ESV)

Luke 9:21-22 And he strictly charged and commanded them to tell this to no one, saying, "The Son of Man must suffer many things and be rejected by the elders and chief priests and scribes, and be killed, and on the third day be raised." (ESV)

1 Timothy 6:17 As for the rich in this present age, charge them not to be haughty, nor to set their hopes on the uncertainty of riches, but on God, who richly provides us with everything to enjoy. (ESV)

Psalm 112:7 He is not afraid of bad news; his heart is firm, trusting in the LORD. (ESV)

CHAPTER 8

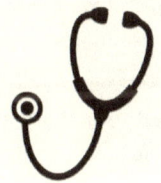

DIAGNOSING THE SHIFT FROM GOD TO A POSSESSION

Let me ask you something that I'm not so sure many people take the time to consider, regardless of their current financial position. Do you need to have nice things to maintain a sense of well-being?

Does the home you live in or the car you drive make you discontent?

How about the brand of the clothes you wear, size of your phone, entertainment system, or even landscaping for curb appeal?

These are symptoms that your faith is shifting from God alone to a possession. Or, said another way, that your faith is shifting from being centered on Jesus to trusting in material belongings. Don't get me wrong, it's alright if the Lord has made us wealthy and enabled us to enjoy many nice possessions. However, it's not okay to trust our nice possessions for our well-being or enjoyment in life.

In fact, you might even be in a position where nice possessions allow you the opportunity to reach a certain group of people. Even so, it becomes a sin issue when you find yourself needing those possessions to experience a sense of well-being. It is the Lord who gives us the grace to enjoy the nice things He gives us (Ecclesiastes 5:19). And it is the Lord who richly provides us with everything to enjoy in the first place (1 Timothy 6:17).

Putting Possessions in Their Place

As a pastor of a church I try to dress in such a way that my clothes don't take attention away from my message or my actions. In other words, I dress with the hope of avoiding drawing attention away from my mission, that is, helping lead people to repent and believe the Gospel, and grow to maturity in Christ.

On that same note, throughout my ministry life, I've tried to drive cars that would not detract from the work I am doing. Just as the Lord might provide us with the funds and the missional environment for owning and leaning on nice things, He may very well place us within a ministry position, a place of employment, or the sports or entertainment industry and not provide the funds for possessions that are on par with those we are among. In that case, the Lord has decided it doesn't matter what people might think about the pedigree of our belongings.

At the end of the day, Christians chasing after Christ in Christlike obedience will be and perform the Lord's will, trusting the results of our life, work, and ministry to Him even if our possessions have the potential of drawing people's attention away from the work the Lord has assigned us. If we trust the Lord alone for our well-being, we'll serve the Lord wholeheartedly, depending upon Him to help us succeed in the ministry He has placed us in.

Let's look at this from another angle.

Suppose you can afford the best possessions, yet the Lord has placed you among the poorest—would you be able to be content living with less than what you could otherwise afford, all for the sake of the Gospel? Listen, if our faith, or trust, is in our possessions, we will likely not take the Lord's assignment to live below what we can afford and, in our place, God will raise up another to reap the blessing He wanted us to have. In that sense, we'll have already received our reward—house, car, clothes, etc.—in place of the true blessing God intended for us.

Possessions cannot sustain our sense of well-being, and God never intended them to. And guess what? We aren't supposed to trust in them. Listen to the Lord's admonition through the Apostle Paul, "As for the rich in this present age, charge them not to be haughty, nor to set their hopes on the uncertainty of riches, but on God, who richly provides us with everything to enjoy (1 Tim. 6:17 ESV).

If we need certain possessions to succeed in the work God has assigned us, then we are trusting possessions and not God alone. As followers of

Jesus, we're to begin, work at, and complete our God-given assignments trusting the Lord to provide the possessions necessary to complete the work He has assigned us. And whether we're experiencing abundance or are in need, He can provide in both common and miraculous ways.

How often do you thank God for the possessions, whether many or few, that He's currently blessed you with?

How often do you come to Him, clear-minded and self-controlled, seeking His will for the best use of the possessions at your disposal for His glory alone?

Do a heart check. Are you trusting in the possessions you own, the possessions you desire, or in Christ alone?

Passages to Reflect On

Ecclesiastes 5:19 Everyone also to whom God has given wealth and possessions and power to enjoy them, and to accept his lot and rejoice in his toil-- this is the gift of God. (ESV)

1 Timothy 6:17 As for the rich in this present age, charge them not to be haughty, nor to set their hopes on the uncertainty of riches, but on God, who richly provides us with everything to enjoy. (ESV)

CHAPTER 9

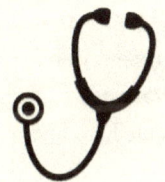

TREATING THE SIN OF A SHIFTED FAITH

Diagnosing the sin of shifted faith to a person, group, event, or possession is far more difficult than implementing the cure. Diagnosis requires time spent in the Word understanding Truth. It requires time in prayer with God the Father. Not to mention it's incredibly beneficial to spend time with trusted believers further along in the faith, partnering with us in our growth. Diagnosis requires our ability to reasonably and faithfully recognize the symptoms while being fully aware of and dependent on the cure.

Yet, even with all that time spent learning to recognize symptoms, the cure itself is relatively simple to implement—repentance and belief. The cure was paid for by the Lord Jesus Christ when he died on the cross, the payment for our sins. When we repent of our shifting faith and believe in Christ, the source of our faith, we're acknowledging that the cure is not only available but that it's accessible here and now.

In Romans 6:23, the author revealed that the wages, or the payment, for sin is death. Christ, on our behalf, paid the cost of sin in full in order to provide the cure for death. In fact, Jesus proclaimed this from the cross in John 19:30 when he said, "It is paid in full!"

I know what you're thinking, that your translation says something like, "It is finished!" and that Jesus didn't say "paid in full" while hanging on the cross. Guess what? The original Greek can be translated either way.

But we also find this teaching on complete and final payment through Christ throughout the New Testament. For instance, Paul wrote in I Corinthians 6:20 that believers have been bought with a price. The price was the life of the Lord Jesus Christ. Peter affirms this in I Peter 1:18-19 by stating we are not ransomed from sin by perishable things but by the blood of Jesus. Jesus did not simply make the first payment on our salvation the way we might a mortgage payment on a house. No, when He paid the price for our sin, He paid the total price, and after paying, He alone was able to proclaim that the payment was complete. That it was finished.

When a believer sins, he or she does not lose their salvation as if they missed a payment on a debt and so lose the car. Our eternal debt is paid! Instead, when we sin, we fall out of fellowship with God. The first of several Milk Doctrines, as I call them, in Hebrews 6 instructs the believer to repent of their dead works, what we call sin (Hebrews 6:1). Repent, as we noted previously, means that we turn away from sin and toward God. When we turn to God, we confess our sin of shifted faith—our dead works—and receive cleansing from all unrighteousness (1 John 1:9).

But we don't stop there. We then ask God to help us put our faith in Him alone. And faith in Christ is the exact opposite of dead works. What's more, John encourages us to pray, noting that if we ask anything according to His will, He hears us and gives us what we ask for (1 John 5:14-15). Do you know what this means for the believer seeking the cure for a shifted faith?

We are cured!

How can we be sure? Because when we attempt to walk by faith in God alone, He fulfills our attempt with His power (2 Thessalonians 1:11).

Just as clogged arteries caused my heart problem, our sin of shifted faith stops the flow of God's resources in our daily life. But repentance for our sin of shifted faith and our subsequent confession opens the flow of God's resources back into our lives just as God miraculously responded to my prayer by cleaning out my arteries and allowing my blood to flow freely through my heart. God's resources flow freely in our life by faith in God (Galatians 2:20). It's that simple. When our faith shifts from God to anything or anyone else, our relationship with Christ shifts, and this relationship-shift hinders the resources God has provided us. When we're cured, that is, when our faith shifts back to Jesus alone, we once again have access to the resources God desires to lavish on us.

How do we treat the sin of shifted faith after it's diagnosed?

1. Repent of it (Hebrews 6:1).

2. Confess it as sin (1 John 1:9).

3. Ask the Lord to draw us back to faith in Him alone (1 John 5:14-15).

In Christ, you and I are new creations, reborn in the way, truth, and life of Christ. But sin easily slips in on us in this sin-enslaved world, doesn't it? So ask yourself regularly, "Has my faith shifted from Christ onto a person, group, event, or possession?" If so, you know what to do.

Before you move on and begin to unpack how to keep your faith in God alone, spend some time reflecting on the following passages. Maybe one or two stood out to you as you worked your way through this chapter. If that's the case, highlight them, write them down, put them to memory and tuck them deep within your heart. Ask the Spirit to open your eyes and ears to Truth and for actionable ways to put Truth into practice in your daily life. Remember to confidently come before the throne. After all, He hears you and is working for your good and His glory.

Passages to Reflect On

Romans 6:23 For the wages of sin is death, but the free gift of God is eternal life in Christ Jesus our Lord. (ESV)

John 19:30 When Jesus had received the sour wine, he said, "It is finished," and he bowed his head and gave up his spirit. (ESV)

1 Corinthians 6:20 for you were bought with a price. So glorify God in your body. (ESV)

1 Peter 1:18-19 knowing that you were ransomed from the futile ways inherited from your forefathers, not with perishable things such as silver or gold, but with the precious blood of Christ, like that of a lamb without blemish or spot. (ESV)

DIAGNOSE SHIFTING FAITH

Hebrews 6:1 Therefore let us leave the elementary doctrine of Christ and go on to maturity, not laying again a foundation of repentance from dead works and of faith toward God, (ESV)

1 John 1:9 If we confess our sins, he is faithful and just to forgive us our sins and to cleanse us from all unrighteousness. (ESV)

1 John 5:14-15 And this is the confidence that we have toward him, that if we ask anything according to his will he hears us. And if we know that he hears us in whatever we ask, we know that we have the requests that we have asked of him. (ESV)

2 Thessalonians 1:11 To this end we always pray for you, that our God may make you worthy of his calling and may fulfill every resolve for good and every work of faith by his power, (ESV)

Galatians 2:20 I have been crucified with Christ. It is no longer I who live, but Christ who lives in me. And the life I now live in the flesh I live by faith in the Son of God, who loved me and gave himself for me. (ESV)

CHAPTER 10

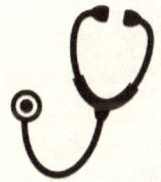

KEEPING
OUR FAITH
IN GOD ALONE

The life of a faithful follower of Christ is wrapped up in Him alone. It's a life that employs the cure for shifting faith as Jesus opens our eyes to the sin that so easily creeps in, shifts, and attempts to destroy. We live this way, wholly reliant on the cure, by faith in the Son of God, who loves us and gave Himself for us.

As maturing believers we understand what a healthy and victorious life in Christ is.

We diagnose our symptoms of a shifted faith to a person, group, event, or possession.

We ask the Lord to reveal what we are trusting in, knowing full well that He will reveal it to us by faith.

We treat sin by repentance, confession to God, and exercising faith in God alone, trusting Him to fulfill our attempt with His power.

And we keep our faith in God alone by repeating this spiritual practice on a regular basis because we know from Scripture and experience the power and perfect love of the One who gave Himself for us.

A Lifetime of Keeping

I know from experience the freedom that comes with turning back to faith in God alone, time and time again. And the ongoing summation of these experiences rooted in the reality of Christ compels me to pass on to you the diagnostic practice of treating, by faith in Jesus, the slippery slide of a shifting faith.

While there are any number of activities, groups, service opportunities, and spiritual practices you might engage in to help keep your focus on, and your faith in, God alone—the primary way is a consistent daily meeting with Jesus in Scripture and in prayer. I can attest that as I've met with Him over the years up until the present, He has revealed and continues to reveal more and more how He has equipped me to live an abundant life and be content in any circumstance. And this isn't just true for me—this is the reality for all who keep their faith in Christ despite circumstances. After all, Jesus did say, "I am with you always, to the very end of the age," didn't He (Mat. 28:20b)?

Think about it, when we daily enjoy the company of those we love and are close to, we get to know them better and better. The same thing happens when we meet daily with the Lord in Word and prayer. We discover more about His Truth, teachings, resources, plans, and purpose for our life and His grand design. In short, we get to know Him better. And the better we know Jesus, the more we trust Him.

It's been fifty-one years now since I put my faith in Jesus. And you know what? Each and every year, I've been privileged to get to know Him better. He loves me with unfailing love. He disciplines me to keep me from being ruined by sin or to prevent me from failing to gain the exhilaration of completing the work He has assigned me. And He keeps His promises.

More than ever, I know when I am thinking, saying, or acting sinfully and that my faith has shifted away from God alone. In the same way that my chest pains caused me to seek out a doctor who clued me into the heart issue affecting my body—my growing spiritual awareness prompts me to get with Jesus quickly to help diagnose where my faith has shifted, repent of it, confess it as sin, and ask the Lord to help me trust in Him alone.

And just as I continue to learn to recognize the symptoms of the heart issues impacting my body and can treat them more quickly and confidently—doing the same in my spiritual life allows me to get back to faith in God alone sooner than I would otherwise and with less damage to myself and those around me. God will do the miraculous to help us walk in the freedom of having our faith in Him alone. He is able to do far beyond what we ask or think according to His power at work in us (Ephesians 3:20, 21).

At the start of this particular journey I had prayed for the urgency to do His work, the work He assigned me in writing about diagnosing shifting faith and its cure. By letting me experience the threat of a major heart attack, I felt the urgency, and by His strength and wisdom, I acted on it. As I sit here today, I'm not only recovered by His grace, but the assignment is also complete.

And while the written portion of my assignment has come to a joyful end, the urgency to help people learn to diagnose when their faith has shifted from God alone and apply the cure of repentance, confession, and asking God to help them get their faith back in Him alone, remains. When we walk by faith in God alone, we shine the light of life in the darkness of sin and show the way for people to be cured of their sins by repenting and believing the Gospel.

What the Lord has taught you in these pages about remedying a shifting faith, He wants you to practice daily. But not just you—as you practice, be sure to pass it on to others as opportunities arise. After all, both Ezra and Paul modeled this lifestyle of passing it on. Throughout history, God has given the Church examples of faith lived and passed on—Ezra in the Old Testament and Paul in the New Testament. Check out the following passages that shed some light on their pass-it-on lifestyles:

> For Ezra had set his heart to study the Law of the LORD, and to do it and to teach his statutes and rules in Israel. (Ezra 7:10 ESV)

> Be imitators of me, as I am of Christ. (1 Corinthians 11:1 ESV)

> ...and what you have heard from me in the presence of many witnesses entrust to faithful men who will be able to teach others also. (2 Timothy 2:2 ESV)

Keep on Keeping on... In Faith

We enter into a relationship with Jesus by grace through faith (Ephesians 2:8-9).

We maintain that fellowship by grace through faith and walk in freedom from sin (2 Corinthians 12:9; Galatians 2:20; Romans 6:6-7).

We do this not because we loved Him but because He first loved us (1 John 4:19).

You can live your life with a Christ-centered sense of well-being. You can walk in the freedom that comes from trusting and obeying God alone. No, this daily spiritual walk isn't just for pastors, professional theologians, or vocational missionaries—it's simply the byproduct of a Christian willing to repent when a shift in faith has been revealed.

Are you ready to diagnose the symptoms of a shifting faith? If not, work your way through the diagnostic chapters once again, spending time on the scriptures offered slowly and with intentionality. Then read through the whole book again until it becomes experiential knowledge ready to be used the moment you begin to recognize symptoms of a shifted faith.

Passages to Reflect On

Ephesians 2:8 For by grace you have been saved through faith. And this is not your own doing; it is the gift of God, 9 not a result of works, so that no one may boast. (ESV)

2 Corinthians 12:9 But he said to me, "My grace is sufficient for you, for my power is made perfect in weakness." Therefore I will boast all the more gladly of my weaknesses, so that the power of Christ may rest upon me. (ESV)

Galatians 2:20 I have been crucified with Christ. It is no longer I who live, but Christ who lives in me. And the life I now live in the flesh I live by faith in the Son of God, who loved me and gave himself for me. (ESV)

Romans 6:6-7 We know that our old self was crucified with him in order that the body of sin might be brought to nothing, so that we would no longer be enslaved to sin. For one who has died has been set free from sin. (ESV)

APPENDIX

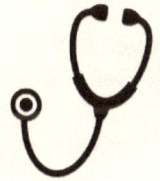

SOME
COMMON
Symptoms

Irritation at _____ (fill in the blank).

Unrighteous anger (angry and sinning in your anger).

Anger at God because things didn't happen as you expected (not trusting God to always be your help—Romans 8:32—and not attributing evil to sin and Satan where it belongs).

Pain and defensiveness when you think someone has insulted you.

Pain and defensiveness when someone rebukes or corrects you.

Sinning to meet a need that is begging to be met instead of waiting on God to meet your need in a righteous way.

Responding to correction by shutting down or lashing out.

Despondent when a sporting event doesn't turn out the way you'd hoped.

Hurt at the loss of fellowship with grandkids.

Hurt by a family member that hinders your joy, peace, production, etc.

Fearful because you think what either you or someone else has said might cause financial, friendship, or some other type of loss, harm, or hurt to your personal well-being.

Fear of a lack of daily provision, which indicates faith in people, health, economy, past decisions, etc.

Being faced with the impossibility of a need being met and choosing to complain about it.

Security in material wealth.

If relations are not right with people and your sense of well-being leaves, then your faith was in the relationship, not in the Lord.

If a person important to you is living or thinking in ways you think are harmful and your sense of well-being is compromised, then your faith is in that person to meet your needs by thinking or living in a particular way.

Trust in government for provision is revealed by voting for a candidate's platform that goes against the Lord, but provides for your provision. (Side note: provision from government is God's provision, just as provision from a job is God's provision, or gifts to a ministry are God's provision.)

The need to defend yourself to maintain a sense of well-being is trusting in your reputation, abilities, or title. (Side note: Defending yourself to help those you serve is sometimes necessary, but is not done to maintain a sense of well-being.)

Appreciation is sought from people to maintain a sense of well-being.

Desiring the praise of people in order to have a sense of well-being.

Discouragement when things don't go how we want them to go to maintain our sense of well-being.

Vengeful thoughts when someone has done something you consider wrong and it ruins your sense of well-being.

Lack of confidence in being and doing what is God's will.

Trusting in yourself (arrogance) as opposed to relying on God alone.

The hurt felt when you are told by a person, "I wouldn't have been in a relationship with you if I had known you better," or any number of variations of this statement.

Anger when you see people not doing what you think is right and responding in an ungodly way to them.

Particular possessions are needed for you to have a sense of peace, joy, or sense of well-being.

Lack of sense of well-being when a person you've sinned against remains cool, aloof, and distant after asking the person to forgive you of your sin against them.

Needing something other than your relationship with Jesus to give you a sense of well-being, joy, peace, hope, etc.

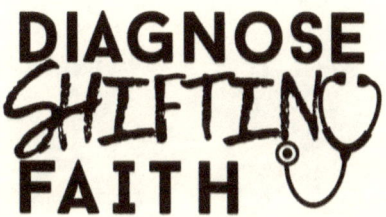

ABOUT RAY HAAS

Ray Haas is an ordinary guy seeking to follow Christ. Matthew 28:19-20 is his life's ambition and confidence. He is continually seeking to learn the Word, live the Word, and pass it on. He is blessed with an excellent wife, three sons, three wonderful daughters-in-law, and ten grandchildren. He lives in the geographical area of God's choosing, hoping to reach those seeking God with the good news of Jesus Christ. His greatest delight is to meet with the Lord daily in the Word and prayer. He has no greater joy than to see people walking in the Truth.

www.ingramcontent.com/pod-product-compliance
Lightning Source LLC
Chambersburg PA
CBHW030457130626
46549CB00007B/2762